T0160207

The
Politically
Incorrect
Success
System

OTHER TITLES BY LARRY WINGET

Get Out of Your Own Way!

Success is Your Own Damn Fault!

The Politically Incorrect Success System

The Politically Incorrect Success System

Larry Winget

MEDIA

Published 2020 by Gildan Media LLC
aka G&D Media
www.GandDmedia.com

Front cover design by David Rheinhardt of Pyrographx

Interior design by Meghan Day Healey of Story Horse, LLC

Library of Congress Cataloging-in-Publication Data is available
upon request

ISBN: 978-1-7225-0525-7

10   9   8   7   6   5   4   3   2   1

Contents

Introduction

This book will introduce you to the Politically Incorrect Success System. Why is it called *politically incorrect*? I have a feeling you're going to figure that out very soon.

My approach is not like that of the typical motivational bozos out there, who want to blow smoke up your skirt and make you feel better about yourself. I don't give a damn how you feel about yourself. That's not what is going to make you successful.

You're going to have to get off your butt and do some things to be successful if you're really serious about changing the results that you have in your life. Now can you already tell that this book is going to be different from the ones you've read in the past?

We have been filled with more happy crap than we have with good ideas that you can take action on to make a real difference in your life, and that's what I want this book to be about. I want you to start to look at things, not through rose-colored glasses, but through a realistic view of your own world—why you have produced the results that you have, and what you can do differently to create new and better results.

I don't pull any punches. If you're being an idiot, I'll tell you you're being an idiot. If you're doing stupid stuff, I'm not here to make you feel good about that. I want to point out to you that you are doing stupid stuff.

My entire philosophy is based on the oldest joke in the world. A guy goes to the doctor, raises his arm, and says, "Doctor, it hurts when I do this." The doctor says, "Well, then, don't do that."

That's what we're going to do in this book. I'm going to show you the stupid things that you have been doing, and I'm going to tell you to stop doing them. It's really that simple.

When I talk about what it takes to be successful, I'm going to be more blunt than people are typically comfortable with. The whole idea of political correctness, which I believe is the most castrating thing that has ever happened to our society, is that we have to say things that never hurt anyone's feelings. We have to use words that dance around a topic or a subject, and we certainly would never want to step on your toes in any way and bruise your fragile, little ego. That's what political correctness has done to us. We can't be truthful. We can't say the way things really are. We always have to be so careful.

I throw all that out the door, and I just say what needs to be said. Some of what needs to be said is that people are doing stupid things and producing stupid results, and then they want to blame someone else for their problems. That doesn't fly with me.

Being politically correct is killing us, so I will be politically incorrect. I will talk to you directly about things going on in society that you have probably slipped into. You've been quite unaware that they're hurting you and your chances of being successful. You haven't even realized that you're doing things that are holding you back.

I want you to shrug off all that political correctness and get real. If you're not able to get real with the world, that's fine, but I want you to at least get real with yourself. I want you to be able to look yourself in the eye in the mirror and have a real conversation in which you use the words that you would if you were with a couple of your best buddies over a beer. You talk to yourself like a real person.

You see, we're so afraid of hurting everybody else's feelings that we've gotten to the point where we're protecting our own feelings. We won't have an honest, direct conversation with ourselves. We have become so tender that we won't say the words we should be saying to ourselves. We will avoid them at all costs simply to protect our own fragile little feelings.

I don't want that to ever happen again. I want you to look yourself in the eye and talk to yourself like a real person. Talk to yourself like the idiot you know you've been. Be honest.

We're running business by focus group. We've even gotten to the point where we're running our personal lives by social media. Everybody has to post, "What do you think of this? What should I do in this situation? Should I break up with him or not? Should I eat this for lunch? This is what I had for lunch. Does it look good to you?"

Who the hell cares? Why don't you live your own life? Why don't you grow a pair in your life to the point where you are confident enough with who you are and the decisions you make that you don't need the yammering of all the idiots out there to approve of what you do?

That's not who we've become. We have to be so careful, so politically correct. We're running everything by appearance, by other people's opinion. I learned a long time ago that I can't pay my bills with somebody else's opinions. I have to have my own opinions.

Right now people are so focused on being politically correct that they are afraid to express themselves. They're afraid to use the words I'm using right here, mainly because we've become such a litigious society. We will sue anybody for anything. I'm amazed at the things that we will sue people for. And we have attorneys out there who will happily take your case to court and take your money for it.

So I understand that somebody in the corporate world might hesitate to say, "I'm just going to throw off all political correctness and go out and do what I want to do and say what I want to say." You have to use your head. You have to understand that you still do work for people. You can't go against the corporate culture, but that doesn't mean that you have to squelch your personality, your belief system, what you stand for, or your core values.

In our culture, we've compromised our core values in order to be politically correct, to get along in the world. We'll go along with anything just in order to get along. But core values are a big deal to me, and I think they are at the very heart of authenticity.

If I walked up to the average guy on the street and said, "Tell me five things you believe in, that you will never compromise, no matter what," he would look at me like a dog looking at a ceiling fan. He would just shake his head and look at me with uncertainty, because we've reached a sad place in society where we don't really know what we believe.

We have to ask someone else. We have to turn on television and hear what our favorite talking head on our news program believes before we're sure about what we believe. Or we have to run it past our buddies on social media, or we have to call and ask somebody to establish what our core values are.

That's a shame. If we don't figure out what our core values are, to the point we will never compromise them for any reason, That's going to lead to the destruction of our society.

If somebody walks up to me and says, "Larry, tell me something you won't compromise no matter what," I'll say, "Honesty." You don't get to lie to me. I mean, you don't get to lie to me. Period. Ever. If you're in business with me, and you lie to me, I will cut you off at the knees, and we are done. I will find somebody else to do business with.

I had a friend for fifteen years, and I caught him in a huge lie. I threw that fifteen years of friendship out the door and said, "No. You've lied to me. Trust has been destroyed. We are done," and I walked away.

People will say, "Where is your forgiving heart?" I don't have a forgiving heart when it comes to dishonesty. We see so much dishonesty, so much misrepresentation out there, and so much that's being said that we know in our hearts isn't true, but we let it slide. We don't speak up. We compromise honesty as a core value.

We'll say, "Sure, we want honesty," but we let dishonesty slide. We let it slide with politicians. We let it slide with our employees, with our friends, with our kids. When we do that, that's dishonesty of our own.

Honesty is a core value that I will never compromise. Others are respect for other people. Doing the right thing, even when it's inconvenient. I could go on and on. I have a lot of core values that I will never compromise, and that's what I ask you to do—establish your core values.

I want to know what you believe in so much that it doesn't matter how loudly I argue against it. If I held a gun to your head and said, "I want you to change your mind," you still wouldn't do it.

If we establish those principles, and we absolutely enforce them, think how quickly we could turn around American business. Think how quickly we could get back on track politically if we just said, "Politicians, you don't get to do this. We will vote your stupid butts out of office. You have been dishonest with us, and we refuse to tolerate it."

Here's what most people don't understand: if you tolerate it, you are condoning it. If you put up with it, you're endorsing it. Look at all the stupidity in the world that we're putting up with, all the things that we are condoning. If we just put our foot down and became politically incorrect and said, "No, you don't get by with that, not with me, you don't," think how we could turn our entire world around.

Can we turn the entire world around? No. I believe the world will change when it wants to change, not because we want it to change. However, you could turn your own personal world around. Your world could be different today if you just said, "These are the lines in the concrete." We used to say "lines in the sand." To hell with that. I'm into lines in the concrete. Those will never, ever be compromised, not in my world.

If you did that, people would treat you differently. People would respect you more. They wouldn't like you more, but they would respect you more, and they would know what your boundaries were.

What if a business said, "Nope, these are our core values"? Businesses call them "mission statements." Mission statements rarely work. Your employees don't know what they are. Your customers certainly don't know what they are.

If a business established core values and said, "This is what we believe in; these are the disciplines that we hold important in our business," and they communicated those values to their customer base and their employees—if they said, "This is what we believe in, this is what we will enforce, and these are the consequences we will impose if these core values are not enforced and lived by"—it would be able to change business.

If you did this, you would attract better employees to you. You would attract employees that adhere to your core values. People wonder why they get stupid employees. It's because your values aren't clear, and you're willing to hire people who are not in alignment with them.

That's what this whole thing is about: establishing what you believe in and becoming uncompromising to the point you won't put up with anything but the best for yourself, at least in your own life. Then you take it from your life to your family. You take it with you wherever you go—to church, to the gym, in traffic, with your friends, on the job. Once you have enough clarity in your life that everyone knows who you are, what you believe in, what you stand for, and what you won't put up with, you will change your life for the better.

We're seeing such growth of entrepreneurs and solopreneurs because, I believe, people desperately want to go back to this core-value living. They're so tired of corporate cultures and societal pressures that they say to themselves, "I want to go out on my own and do this my way."

It's exciting for our country that we have such a boom among solopreneurs and entrepreneurs. But always remember this: keep your day job until you figure out how to provide enough value in the marketplace that you can earn a living by being an entrepreneur. The key to this is always: how much value can I add in the marketplace?

Often people want to go into business and say, "I'm tired of the business world. I'm tired of the corporate culture. I'm tired of working for the man. I'm tired of working for somebody else. I'm going to do this on my own," and they don't have a clue what they're doing. They haven't done a darn thing to prepare themselves. Instead they have a passion. Well, passion doesn't get you paid. Hard work gets you paid. Being good at what you do gets you paid. Hard work and excellence and providing a lot of value. Your customers don't pay for your passion.

When I start to attack passion, that's politically incorrect, because you have all these bozos who create pretty little signs, these little memes, and put them on Facebook. Just because they have a gorgeous sunset in the back and say, "Follow your passion," people think that's what they ought to click and like and share, and that's how they ought to live their lives.

No. I lose business because I attack passion. People love to hear that their business should be based on passion, not understanding that passion is defined in the dictionary as *uncontrollable emotion.* Why would you want an uncontrollable emotion anywhere near your business? I don't understand that.

I was hired to do to an after-dinner speech. I don't do a lot of after-dinner speeches at this point in my career. I do a lot of morning speeches and kick-offs for associations, but this was an after-dinner speech, and they had a lot of money. I'm politically incorrect enough to say that I do this because I'm good at it, and they pay me a lot to do it.

So I was happy to do this guy's after-dinner speech. I typically don't hang with an audience. I'm not good that that. I understand what my strengths and weaknesses are. I'm not good at the one-on-one stuff. I love people; it's individuals I have issues with.

So I did the after-dinner speech. On my way back to my room, I stopped by the bar. I was the only guy there. They were all still in their meeting. I sat over in the corner by myself, sipping a bourbon before I went to my room and went to bed so I could leave the next morning.

Here they came. The president of the company came over to me and said, "Larry, I want to thank you for the passion you shared with my people tonight."

I said, "I apologize if you saw any passion at all."

"Oh, Larry," he said, "I know you're kidding me here. We saw a lot of passion tonight."

"I can assure you, you didn't see any passion," I said. "You're probably just not used to seeing a guy who is really good at what he does for a living. You saw a guy who's good at what he does for a living. I'm excellent. I work hard at it. It took me a lot of years to get this good. That's what you saw, but you didn't see any passion."

He laughed again and said, "Oh, Larry, I know you're just kidding. That's something you just like to say. It's part of your brand."

"Let me be real clear," I said. "My passion is sitting on my back patio watching the sun go down over the mountain with a good bourbon in my left hand, a good cigar in my right hand, my bulldog sitting on my lap, and my wife sitting in the chair next to me, with Merle Haggard playing in the background. *That's* my passion. *This* is my work. I want to thank you for helping finance my passion, because that's what you're doing."

I do what I do because I have worked hard to become one of the best at it. I have achieved excellence in my field, not because I am passionate but because I am committed to providing great value to my customers. We have too many people going into business today purely because they're passionate about something, and the sad thing is they're not any good at it.

Years ago on *The Big Idea with Donny Deutsch* show on CNBC, he would have a person who came on at the end for a segment called "The Millionaire Minute" and talk about the topic of the day. Wouldn't you know? The day that I got there, the topic of the day was passion. Donny said, "Larry, tell me how you feel about passion."

I said, "Donny, I think passion is a total load of crap." You could just see Donny go all pale underneath his orange makeup.

He said, "Larry, I disagree."

"Donny, you can disagree if you want to," I said. "It is your television show. You have every right to be wrong."

"Larry, passion is the key."

"No," I said. "Let me get real clear about the keys to success. Hard work and excellence are the keys to success. Just hard work and excellence." That's what it's always going to come down to: hard work and excellence. The problem is, people try only one of those.

For years, we heard that excellence was the key. Tom Peters wrote a book called *In Search of Excellence.* Everybody focused on excellence. I know people who are excellent at what they do, but they don't work hard enough at it for it to make any difference.

On the other hand, people think hard work is the key. I am a huge believer in hard work, but I know people who work really hard at what they do, and they're just not any good at it. So it doesn't make any difference.

It's the combination of hard work and excellence that makes the difference—with a commitment to always be better at what you do and provide more value to the marketplace, because we are ultimately rewarded for our value, not for our passion.

If you're in a hospital, lying in the surgical suite, about to have a quadruple bypass, and they bring the surgeons out and say, "You're about to have a quadruple bypass on your heart. We have a surgeon who is really passionate about cutting people open, and we have another surgeon who is damn good at what he does," I'll take the surgeon who's damn good at what he does. I don't want a guy who's passionate about cutting people open. I'm not paying for passion.

When your life or your business depends on it, you'll go with hard work and excellence, not passion. So let's get that passion and that political correctness and that feel-good crap out of the way right now and get down to what it really takes to be successful. It's going to come down to you working harder at what you do and being better at it.

In Steven Pressfield's book *The War of Art*, he talks about people who love what they do—in essence are passionate about what they do. He said the amateur loves what they do, but the professional loves what they do enough to become the best at it. Are you going to be an amateur who's only passionate and who only loves what they do for a living, or are you going to become a professional who loves it enough to become the best at it?

A Tibetan proverb says, "It is better to live one day as a tiger than to live for a thousand years as a sheep." Many people today are living their lives as sheep, following the herd. Whatever the herd is doing, that's what we'll do. We never want to step away from the herd, step into our own excellence, accept it, and speak up on behalf of ourselves, because that would mean that we would be different.

You're going to have to be different. You're going to have to be the one tiger in the herd of sheep if you really want to be successful, both personally and in business.

Being the person who steps out, who doesn't look like the herd, who is willing to stand up for everything they believe—well, that has some side effects. It has some positive side effects, and some negative ones.

Let me tell you what will happen to you if you decide to live more politically incorrectly and embrace the fullness of your own excellence. First, you will discover that you are more successful. Successful people in business, in any area of life—even if you're one of those spiritual people who wants to throw business to the side and say it's not about money, it's about achieving a higher plan—those people don't follow the herd. All the people who have ever made it throughout history have been people who have stepped away from the herd and have been tigers.

You want to talk about music? The biggest tiger we ever had in the history of music was Elvis Presley. You want to talk about the history of the world? The biggest tiger in history was Jesus. There's a person who stepped away from the herd. He wasn't a sheep. He was a leader of sheep. He was the person who stepped away.

Our great business leaders and political leaders have been willing to step into themselves, step into their greatness, and speak up on behalf of their core values and what they really believe. Most people simply aren't willing to do that. If you do, you will achieve more success simply because people are attracted to you. You will attract more customers. You will attract better employees. You will be more attractive in the marketplace, in relationships, in every area of your life, because you have confidence.

The most attractive thing on this planet is confidence. We all love confident people. It's the most attractive thing in relationships. A man loves confidence in a woman. When my wife gets up in the morning, fixes her hair, puts on her favorite outfit, looks herself in the mirror, smiles at herself, gives herself a little wink, and knows she looks good, that's when she looks best to me. A man who carries himself with confidence, walks tall and straight, and speaks up for who he is, is attractive. People want to be around that kind of person. These are the great leaders in society, in business, in music, in churches, in history, in politics. They're people who know how to do that.

So you're going to achieve more success and become more attractive to people. You'll have more confidence simply because you have the freedom to be who you really are and not just one of the many. Nobody is attracted to one of the many. Being one of the many means that you're mediocre. You're right in the middle. You're average. Who wants to be average? Average doesn't make any money. There's no money in average. There's always money in being the unique one that steps away. There's always freedom in that. That's what you really want.

You'll start to get better service too. That's one of the things I like the best. I'm a person who speaks up and is very clear that I won't put up with bad service. I get better service because people know I won't put up with it. I don't look or carry myself or talk like the kind of guy that you want to screw over. People treat me right because they go, "Oh, this guy is probably going to be a pain in the butt if I don't give him good service. He'll probably talk to me about it. He'll probably call my manager about it.

He'll probably hold me accountable for my actions. He will probably impose consequences on me."

A guy set an appointment with me to sell me garage doors. I said, "You pick the appointment. I don't care; I'm free all day. Tell me what time you will be here, but be here. That's all I'm asking. Be here at 10:00."

He said, "I can be there at 10:00, 10:00 is perfect for me. I have nothing else going on." At 11:30, he rang my doorbell, and he said, "Here I am."

I said, "You were supposed to be here at 10:00."

"I got a little held up," he said.

"Is your phone broken? You couldn't get to the phone? Did you know at 9:45 that you were going to be held up, and you weren't going to make your 10:00 appointment? You knew in advance you were going to be late. Why didn't you let me know?"

"I didn't figure it'd make that much difference."

"It makes a difference." I said. "We're not doing business. Have a good day."

"Wait, wait, wait," he said. "I sell the best garage doors in the city. Why wouldn't you want to do business with me?"

"Because you can't keep your word. You don't respect me enough to show up on time. You don't respect yourself enough as a professional to make a phone call to let me know you're running late. If you can't show up on time for your appointment, I don't trust you to install good product."

"That's not fair."

"I don't have to be fair. I'm the customer. It's my money. I don't have to be fair."

I'm the kind of guy that you don't want to treat badly because I have such strength in my position, my point of view, my core values that I pretty much get good service. You'll get better service when you step into that and start to speak up and stand up for yourself.

You'll also have better friends, because you'll become intolerant of the idiots that you have surrounded yourself with. Understand this too: you want more money; everybody says they want more money. If you do, understand this: your income right now is an average of the incomes of your five closest friends. So think of your five best buddies. You know about how much money they make. Add that up and average it. That's how much money you make.

Now you may be saying, "I need to get richer friends." Yeah, you probably do. You may also be saying, "My friends mean more to me than that." Listen, if your friends are holding you back from being the best version of yourself, they are not your friends. Dump them. Walk away from them. They are not moving you closer to your goals, and if they are not moving you closer to your goals, they are moving you farther away from your goals, and they are not your friends. Anybody who holds you back is not your friend.

When you become clear about who you are and have absolute clarity in your core values, you step into it. You talk about it. You live it. You express it in every way through your very being. You're clear about yourself. You will attract better friends into your life. You will have more to talk about. You will talk less about people and more about important things. Your income will go up, I promise. You will have more money simply because you have elevated your self-awareness, the quality of the people you surround yourself with, and your respect for the people you work for and the customers you serve. Your income will reflect that.

Here's another big benefit of absolute clarity in your life: you will have better children. Your kids are a reflection of you. If you're sloppy, chances are your kids are going to be sloppy. If you're fat, chances are you've got fat kids. If you don't read, your kids won't read. If you watch television all evening, don't be surprised when your kids want a TV in their bedroom (which, by the way, you've probably already given them). Don't be surprised when they want to sit on their butts and watch television all the time too. If you don't go outside, they won't go outside. If you don't exercise, they won't exercise.

When you become a better person, more confident in yourself, and very clear about what you believe, your kids will start to become clear in their own lives. Their confidence will increase. You will be a better parent, meaning that you will have better kids.

The rewards of stepping up and living a politically incorrect life are huge. Who wouldn't want more friends, more money, a better life, better kids, a better job, more satisfaction, more happiness, more confidence? The rewards far outweigh the downside, but there is a downside: when you decide to live the kind of life that I've described, you're going to experience criticism. People are going to start to criticize you for the way you live.

Let's be clear. The only way to avoid criticism is to be nothing, do nothing, and say nothing, because anything you do or say, you will be criticized for. Everything will bring criticism.

I get criticism every single day. I don't care. It doesn't bother me that people want to criticize what I have to say. I am above that. I have risen above the approval of other people.

You need to stop looking to others for approval. We've become so needy. We want everybody to love everything that we do. When we get up in the morning, the first thing we do is take a picture of our breakfast and put it on Facebook so we can get feedback from other people: "Oh, that looks so good. Honey, you're so lucky. I bet that shake is amazing. I bet those eggs were perfect."

Why do you care? Get past that. Why are you so needy that you want everybody to approve of what you do? Here's the problem: people overshare. Don't be guilty of oversharing. How do you know if you overshare? Go back and count how many times you post pictures on Facebook looking for people to tell you your kids are cute, to tell you, "Oh, that looks good, I wish I was where you are today. I wish I was eating that today."

You're seeking the approval of other people. A little bit of that is fine, but if you're oversharing, it's because you lack self-confidence. It's because your ego needs to be stroked, and you want other people to like you. Let me tell you right now: you'll be much better off in life if people respect you for the strength of your point of view, for the strength of your convictions, for the strength of how you act out your core beliefs in every area of your life. That's respect.

Everything else is just having fun, I guess, because there's no other reason for you to be needy and want everybody to love you and stroke your ego. Stop being weak, and become strong. Stop needing everybody else's approval.

If you live and die for the approval of other people, it's sad, but that's what we've created in our society right now. That's that politically correct society, where we have to please everyone. If that's what matters most to you, this is going to be a problem for you, because you have to understand you will receive criticism, and you're going to have to learn to be OK with it.

You see, when we become afraid of what other people say about us, that's when we've given them all of our power, and do you want to admit to yourself that you've give up all of your power?

Right now, there are problems with bullying and lawsuits and so on because people are using words to hurt the feelings of other people. Words. I grew up hearing the same little thing you did: sticks and stone may break my bones, but words will never hurt me. What happened to that? They're just words, and typically they're words from people you don't give a damn about to begin with, so what does it matter what they say about you?

Cyberbullying. I don't even understand that concept. Somebody goes on the Internet and says something bad about you. Big wah. Who cares? It's just some idiot with Internet balls who would never have the guts to look you in the face and say that to you. You know they wouldn't. They wouldn't say that to your face, but they'll go on the Internet and anonymously type something, and all of a sudden your feelings are crushed.

Kids are killing themselves over that, because their parents haven't taught them the importance of being strong in who they are, and they've put their own feelings up for the approval of other people. We have to get past that. We have to get past the approval of other people. We have to get to the point that we understand that words are just words.

A strong person, a person who has great self-confidence, great self-esteem, doesn't care what other people say, because they know that's just one more stupid person who doesn't have the guts to do what they've done and is speaking out of fear and envy.

Do not give your power up to someone else by letting their words affect you like that, but it will happen that people are going to say bad things about you.

Let me tell you what else. You're going to be called mean. I get called mean.

I was at a party, and I walked through the crowd. I have pretty good hearing, and as I walked through crowd past some people, I heard one woman turn to another couple that was standing with her and say, "That's Larry Winget. He's really mean."

I stopped dead in my tracks, turned around, looked at her, and said, "You don't even know me. I have no clue who you are. How dare you say I'm mean?"

"I see the things you say on television," she said. "I've read one of your books. I see what you say on the Internet, on social media. I think you're mean."

"You know," I said, "it's a damn shame in life when we've reached the point that we call people mean for speaking their truth. I've never put anyone else down for being who they are. I will attack their ideas, I will attack their actions, but I never attack people. I attack actions, results. That's what I go after. Why am I mean for speaking my truth? Have I ever been mean to you?"

She said, "No, you don't even know me."

"Then why am I mean for being truthful?" She had nothing at that point.

That's another thing. A confident person will turn around and confront. Are you going to be confrontational? In other words, are you going to be uncompromising in your beliefs? Are you going to let somebody say you're mean, and have it hurt your feelings and cause you to draw back? It'll cause you to stop being strong. Don't do that. You're going to be called mean. You're going to be called a bully. I get called that a lot. "You're a bully, Larry." No, I'm not. I lift as many people up as I can. But my tactics and style are different. I'm not a person who will blow smoke up your skirt in order to make you feel better about yourself.

I believe that we make people better by holding them accountable so they see the consequences of their actions and their ideas, and of their lack of action. That's the way I make people better. Does that make people uncomfortable? Yes, but we grow when we're uncomfortable, not when we're comfortable. When everything's going perfectly, we don't grow much. When we start to get uncomfortable, to feel a little pain, we'll do anything to resist that discomfort. That's when growth happens. I believe it is my job, my calling, to make people uncomfortable. And believe me, if you step into the way of living I'm talking about, other people will become uncomfortable around you. You have done your job if you make people uncomfortable by living an admirable life. That's a good thing. Be OK with that.

At this point you might be saying, "Larry, that works for you. You're that kind of person. That's probably how you were raised to be that way."

It's true. It does work for me, and I was raised to be confident. I had parents who taught me to be confident and speak up for myself in any situation. I'm very fortunate in that respect, but it's not too late for you, and don't think that you have to be a big guy with biker tattoos and earrings and a motor-cycle to be able to speak up for yourself.

I can show you eighty-pound grandmothers you wouldn't dare cross, simply because they have this aura about them that says, "Don't mess with me. I'll hurt you." That might be *your* grandma. I can show you children in wheelchairs whom nobody messes with. Nobody would bully them, simply because they have confidence in who they are and they carry themselves with such confidence that they don't get bullied.

Life is about being a victim or being in charge. Are you going to be a victim, or are you going to be in charge of your life? Stop being a victim.

And it's not about being a man, being a woman, being young, being old, being big. None of those things matter. I wrote a book called *Grow a Pair*, and I had to explain what I meant. Again, that's a politically incorrect title, and people went after me, saying, "Larry, only men can grow a pair."

"No," I said, "it's not about men growing a pair. Growing a pair is not what's happening between your legs; it's what's happening between your ears. It's about being mentally strong. It's about knowing how to stand up for yourself, first in your mind, and then by carrying it through how you walk, through your choice of vocabulary."

In the next chapter I'll talk about the things you can do to change in your own life that will have an impact on your world, but let's be clear right now. This choice is up to you, and don't use the fact that you're old or a female or young or in college or whatever as a reason you can't do this. Everyone can do this.

1
Fix Yourself First

One challenge in living the politically incorrect life is that we start to become strong, and then we want to criticize and blame everything that's going on outside of our lives. People finally get an opinion and say, "I'm going to be strong and express that opinion," and then they attack the government. They say the government is overspending; the government is trillions of dollars in debt. They don't understand that 43 percent of Americans spend more money than they earn. We hold our government to a higher standard than we hold our own family to. That's not right.

We start to criticize our boss, say, "If my boss wasn't so mealy-mouthed, if he would stand up for what the company really believed in, and would do his job, I would have a better life. I've gotten strong, and now I'm going to criticize my boss."

Or husbands want to blame their wives for their lousy relationship, and wives want to blame their husbands. We might like to blame our kids, but no, we won't blame our kids; our kids can do no wrong. The problem is the school system, or the government. I wrote a book called *Your Kids Are Your Own Fault.* Your kids are a reflection of you.

Some people blame the weather for the fact they're not doing well. "It's been a really cold winter, Larry," or "We have global warming, Larry. If it weren't so darn hot . . ." People will grasp at straws to blame anything outside of themselves. They want to fix everything outside of themselves. But if you want to change your world, it starts here with you. You have to fix yourself first. That is the hardest thing for people to do, because it has become so easy to lay the blame outside of ourselves.

I shot a television show for a few years on A&E called *Big Spender,* and I would go into people's homes and talk to them about their financial situation. Now these were people who volunteered to be on the television show. They knew what I did. They knew that I was going to confront them about their spending problems. They knew I was going to hold them accountable, and there were people who were really a mess. I would go into their homes, and in my warm, sweet, nurturing way, I would point out the error of their ways.

I walked into the home of a woman who had fifty-seven credit cards and hundreds of thousands of dollars in credit-card debt, mostly on shoes, purses, and clothes. She had rooms and rooms full of racks of clothes, and over 500 pairs of shoes. She made $35,000 a year, and her husband delivered pizza for a living. Yet she lived this kind of lifestyle.

When I walked in the door and confronted her, she turned on me, put her finger in my face, and said, "Don't you dare yell at me. This is not my fault. If you want to yell at somebody, call the credit-card companies, because if they would quit sending them to me, I would quit maxing them out."

That's how people think. They don't want to realize that they are the cause of their problems. But you *are* the cause of your problem.

I've written six best sellers. I've been on television, giving my commentary on life and business and parenting and success, and on the whole wussification of America. I can sum up all that I've done in nearly twenty-five years in the personal-development industry with one line: *Your life is your own damn fault.* That's it. Your thoughts, your words, your actions created the life that you are living.

Let's say you were walking along and a tree fell on your head, and you say that's why your life is the way it is. But even if you are not the cause of the way your life is, how you react to what happened to you, that's your fault. At some point, it always comes down to personal responsibility, but many of us are quick to say, "That doesn't apply to me. I am the exception to the rule."

I do speak in generalizations. When I give out statistics saying that 43 percent of people spend more money than they make, I don't make those things up. That's just how it is. You say, "But I don't spend more money than I make." OK, you are the exception to the rule.

When I say two-thirds of people haven't done anything to prepare for retirement, it's true. Then you come back with "But Larry, I did prepare for retirement. You're not talking to me." OK, maybe you're the exception to the rule.

However, we've become way too prone to believing that we are the exception to the rule. So before you decide that you are the exception, I want you to understand this. People who consider themselves the exception to the rule need to go back and reread the rule. Maybe you're not the exception that you want to believe you are.

Be open to what I'm saying, and believe that just maybe this does apply to you. At some point in your life, if you're ever going to move forward, if you're ever going to achieve more in your life, have more money, happiness, better relationships, you're going to have to first understand that as a starting place, you have to take responsibility. The results that you have achieved so far in your life are the consequences of the actions that you have taken.

Still don't believe me? Still think that what I'm talking about doesn't apply to you? Let me give you a series of questions that you can answer. They may give you a better look into yourself and whether you really need to step up and live the kind of life I'm talking about.

The first question is this: do people take advantage of you? Do they push ahead of you in line, and you don't say anything? Do your coworkers slough their work off on you? Do you take it?

Why do you take it? What are you afraid of? Why are you so afraid to speak up? Why are you so afraid to put boundaries in your life?

When you go out to eat, do you eat cold food because you won't say anything to the waiter and send it back? When I say this, people respond, "Larry, they might spit in my food." Well, OK: you can live life afraid that something horrible is going to happen every time that you speak up, but why do you put up with that stuff? I'm not going to play victim to the world by being unwilling to stand up for myself.

Do you let people around you talk in a movie theater? Every time I say this one, people say, "Larry, do you know what happens in movie theaters? People might shoot you." Oh, come on. You are more likely to get hit by lightning than you are to die by going to the movies and telling some idiot in front of you to turn off his cell phone and be quiet.

Get realistic. Could something horrible happen? Yes. You could walk out the door of your office today, step off the curb, trip, fall, break your neck, and end up a quadriplegic. Is it going to happen? Probably not. Yes, there are extremes. Yes, something horrible could happen. Will it probably happen? No.

Ask yourself these tough questions: Why do you let people take advantage of you? Why do you let people push you around? Why won't speak up for yourself? Do you let your friends hurt your feelings and get by with it? Why do you that? Why don't you think more of yourself than that? Do you find yourself unwilling to express yourself, to speak up, to say what you really believe because you're afraid that somebody will be offended?

Somebody is always going to be offended. Somebody's always going to take offense at something you say, no matter what it is. Jesus told people to love one another, and they killed him for it, so I don't care what it is in the world you want to stand up for, somebody's going to put you down for it.

Let's give them a lot to work with. I'm fine with that. You need to become fine with it too. You can't constantly be afraid to express yourself simply because somebody else might become offended.

By the way, if you're one of those people who in the past has become offended, get over it. Words offend you? Get over it.

Do you ever feel like you're being used? Do you ever let people talk down to you? Let me ask you this. Do your kids talk back to you? Oh, now it just got ugly, didn't it? Because that's the one: "Yes, I let my kids talk back to me." If your kids talk back to you, let me just go way out on a limb and say you're a lousy parent. You are a lousy parent if you let your children disrespect you, because allowing a child to disrespect their parent means that you are teaching them that disrespectful behavior is OK and will be tolerated in the home. Don't be surprised when you have crippled your child to the point that when they go into the real world, they don't do well in the workplace, because a disrespectful child at home will become a disrespectful child in the schoolroom, and then in the workplace.

A woman wrote me a letter and said, "I am dealing with a disrespectful sixteen-year-old. He's out of control." I wrote back and said, "He was out of control at sixteen months old. You didn't do anything about it then. It's going to be a lot harder to do something about it now."

Has this little list of questions that I've just given you revealed something to you about how strong you really are? What if I walk up to you and say, "Hey, are you a strong person? Do you speak up for yourself?"

Most people would say, "Sure, I'm that kind of person right now. I don't need this. Larry, I'm already the strong guy that you're talking about. I'm the strong woman. Do you know what I've achieved?" Yeah, OK. But if you don't like your answers to that list, see if you are this kind of person.

When you're facing conflict, do you stand up for yourself? When you're out there, and you see somebody weaker than you being taken advantage of, do you speak up on their behalf? It's amazing the number of people who will not speak up for others for fear of getting involved.

Just recently in the city where I live, two trucks went into a canal full of water. A guy came running up, saw the people drowning in the truck, and asked the others observers to help him. They said, "We don't know those people." That is a shame. He jumped in by himself and held the head of one of the drivers above water so he wouldn't drown.

Are you a person who doesn't want to become involved simply because it takes too much time, it takes too much trouble, fear of the consequences? "If I help, I might get sued. If I help, something bad might happen to me." Or do you get out there and get involved and speak up on behalf of people who can't speak up for themselves?

How do you feel about the mistreatment of others, the mistreatment of animals? Do you speak up on their behalf? I hope you do, because if you're doing the kind of things I'm talking about right now, you're the kind of person that this book can only make better. You're the kind of person who's doing the right thing. Now you can tweak the way you are to become the kind of person who lives full-out and achieves more success.

When you get up in the morning, do you feel a sense of purpose: "I am here for a reason, I'm here to do great things"? Or are you a person who just rolls out of bed and says, "Another lousy, crappy day I have to go out there and live. I hope I can make it to the end of the day without falling asleep. I have to work with those idiots, and then come home and put up with my wife and my kids, and watch a little TV until it's time to go to bed one more time. Tomorrow I'll do it all again"? Is that the kind of person you are? Sadly, that's how most people are.

It's not that you have to do grandiose things. I don't care what your job is. You can still wake up with a sense of purpose. It doesn't matter how you view your job if you view your life with a sense of purpose.

Do you recognize your problems as problems, but understand that problems happen to everybody? You don't feel special; you don't feel victimized by your problems. You say, "Here's a problem. I'm going to tackle it. I can break it down, I can go to work on it, and I can fix this. Give it enough time and enough determination, and I can do something about it."

Do you understand that sometimes life just sucks, and you're the one who has to suck it up and get over it? That's how life is, folks. If you're the kind of person I've just described in the last few pages, you're the kind of person that everybody should be more like. You're the kind of person who already has a strong sense of self. You can build on that and become more and do more and achieve more in your life. It all starts with you and understanding who you are. Once you've done that, you can really start to do amazing things.

That's really step one. Stop blaming. Whenever something happens to you, go to the mirror, look yourself in the eye, and say, "I am the cause of this. What do I need to change in my behavior, the way I talk, the way I act, the things that I do that would bring about different results?" That's what taking responsibility is really about. That's what stopping the blame is really about—when you start to look to yourself first instead of last.

Now let's talk about some other things you can do to make yourself the kind of person that we've been talking about. The next is motive. Ask yourself why you do what you do. If you wake up in the morning with a compelling need to make everybody who surrounds you happy, you're going to be miserable. If there's one thing I've discovered after being around for as long as I have, it's that you're not going to make everybody happy.

It's sad to be a person who feels compelled to make everybody in the world happy. I'm selfish, and I'm a hedonist. But after many years, I also understand that if I wake up and my goal is to make *me* happy, I will make other people happy. I will make other people happy by making me happy. I am happiest when I'm doing what I am supposed to do. I am happiest when I am doing the right thing. I am happiest when I am bringing value to my customers. I am happiest when I'm making my wife happy. I'm happy when I'm being a good parent. My being a good parent doesn't always make my kids happy, but it makes me happy, and ultimately it's always going to be the right thing to do.

My being the right kind of person and telling you the truth in this book is not going to make everybody happy, but if my goal had been to make you happy, I wouldn't say these things. Instead my goal is to fulfill my purpose and my strength, to give you the best of who I am, so those of you who choose to participate can live a better life.

Understand that some people will choose to join you in your glory, in your being the best, in living full-out, and some people won't. Be OK with that. The sad thing is too many of us are trying to win over people we're never going to win over.

Some people aren't going to like you no matter what you do. You can't make them happy. In fact, I don't want somebody trying to make me happy. Nothing in the world bothers me as much as somebody trying to make me happy. Don't be one of those people, and you know whom I'm talking about. Every office has one, every association has one, every circle of friends has one—a little Suzy Sweetcheeks kind of person who runs up to you and says, "Is Mr. Grumpy having a bad day?" Get the hell out of my face. I have stuff to do.

This kind of person wants to make sure that everybody in the world is happy. It's impossible. The quickest way to living a miserable life is to try to make everyone happy. It can't be done.

Here's the next step in fixing yourself. Stop being so willing to compromise, and call right right and wrong wrong. Most people live in a very gray area. I don't have much gray in my life. I live in a black-and-white world. I believe things are either right or wrong. As Les Brown said years ago, "It's right or wrong. It's good or bad. It's hello or goodbye. You're either in the way or on the way." I believe that's true. There's no gray that I choose to participate in.

I'm not denying that there is gray; I'm not denying that there's a place where things can go either way. I'm saying that people who live in the gray are going to live a miserable lives. It's much simpler to say, "This is the right thing to do. This is the wrong thing to do."

This comes down to good decision making. How do you learn to make good decisions? By making a lot of bad decisions. You learn. Don't worry so much about making the right decision. Just make it, and then do everything in your power to make sure that it is the right one. I don't believe we should spend a whole lot of time always trying to decide, is this the thing I should do, is this the thing I shouldn't do?

Every single time, your gut tells you what the right thing to do is. Go with your gut. Is this the right thing to say? Should I tell this joke? If you have to ask yourself, "Should I tell this joke?" if you have to look over your shoulder or look around and say, "I wonder if I can get by with this," you can't. You always know the right thing to do and the wrong thing to do.

Here's another little test you can give yourself: would you want your mama to hear you? That'll do it for you right there. I might disrespect you; I wouldn't disrespect my mama. That's a question you can ask yourself.

You know the right thing to do. You know the wrong thing to do. Don't be a person who hesitates to call it. I never do; I know instantly how I feel about things. I know whether it's the right thing or the wrong thing to do. I'm not saying it's the right thing for *you*; I'm saying it's the right thing for *me*. That's because I have a commitment to my core beliefs.

Unfortunately, we do everything in our power to avoid conflict. Conflict is a natural part of life. I know parents right now who are afraid—I mean *afraid*—to turn the television off, because their kid would be upset if they did. I know parents who are afraid to take their child's cell phone away from them because it would upset the child.

I got a letter from a woman who said, "I can't afford to pay the cell-phone bills of my two teenage daughters anymore, but I would rather be late on my house payment and destroy my personal credit than disappoint my two daughters and have them be underprivileged in the eyes of their friends."

Are you kidding me? You are afraid to tell your daughters you can't afford to pay their cell-phone bills? That's a luxury. It's not a necessity; you can live without it; I did. You'll be just fine. Chances are you did too, but you're afraid to be honest with your daughters, but you're also afraid to destroy your credit history. That's a shame.

I know people who go to work every day and sit beside the biggest jerk in the world. They let that jerk treat them like crap instead of turning around and saying, "Excuse me, I'm better than that. You don't get to talk to me like that."

I know people who put up with friends who verbally abuse them. They take way too much crap from those people when they ought to say, "I'm better than that, and if you can't treat me better and stop disrespecting me, we can't be around each other anymore."

Typically people are afraid of conflict because they're not equipped for the fight. They haven't prepared themselves mentally to be able to speak the words that need to come out of their mouths. If you have to practice those words, if you have to stand in front of a mirror and practice the words you need to say to your kids, to your coworker, to that person who calls himself a friend, to that abusive parent (and there are abusive parents out there), to the people in your life that you need to speak up to, then practice the words to make sure you can get them out. Go into the fight equipped. Don't cripple yourself and leave yourself in a vulnerable position because you're acting by the seat of your pants. Prepare yourself. Everybody has to prepare before they enter the fight.

Some people will say, "Why does life have to be about conflict, Larry? Why can't we all just get along?" Because it's life. We don't all get along.

There are some people you need to say no to. You need to say, "Step back. You don't get to treat me like this. I don't choose to have you participate in my life. I want you to go away."

Now that does take a pair. It takes preparing yourself mentally to handle what happens after you say the words, but you also have to be able to say the words. You have to prepare yourself. Conflict is a natural part of life. It's always going to be there.

You also have to be willing to be judgmental. I take a lot of heat for telling people to become more judgmental. People love to quote the Bible and say, "We're told not to be judgmental." Actually, we're not. Go back and read the entire statement, because it says, "Judge not, lest ye be judged, because by the same measure you judge others, you in turn will be judged" (Matthew 7:1–2).

In other words, if I judge you for spending too much money and being too much in debt, you get to turn around and judge me by that same measure. I'm willing for you to do that. It's OK that I judge you, because I am willing to be judged in the same way.

I make my living being judgmental, saying, "This is right, this is wrong. This is a good idea, this is a bad idea. Stop doing this, start doing that." That's how I live my life, but do you think you don't? Have you ever cast a vote? If you've cast a vote, you were being judgmental. You were choosing one candidate over the other based on whatever criteria.

Have you ever been to a grocery store? Why did you go to that store? Why didn't you go to another one? Because you were judging one store to be better than the other. Why do you go to that restaurant and like their spaghetti instead of the restaurant down the street and their spaghetti? It's because you like that spaghetti better. You judged.

We all judge every single day. People get on their high horse and say, "I'm never going to judge." I'll tell you right now, you're going to be a lousy boss, because it's your job as a boss to judge the behavior of your employees. It is your job as a boss to judge whether your customers are getting the kind of service that they're paying for.

If you're not willing to judge, you're a lousy parent, because it is your job to judge good behavior, bad behavior, what is acceptable, what isn't acceptable. If you never judge the behavior of your kids, you're going to have out-of-control, lousy kids.

So being judgmental is a good thing. Just understand that you are setting yourself up to be judged in the same way. I'm good with that. Are you? If not, fix yourself so it's OK for you to judge, because you're willing to be judged. How's that for an idea?

2
Values and Boundaries

Up to now, we've talked about the problem. Let's now move more into solutions. Let's talk about some of the things that you can actually do in order to make these changes come about.

We are all susceptible to role models in our lives, so start to look at the people who have been your role models—people that you admire for their ability to stand up for themselves, to live life full out, to rise above the approval of other people, to be politically incorrect by today's standards.

For me it's pretty easy. I was raised well. My mama and daddy taught me right and wrong. They taught me what would be acceptable and what wasn't going to be acceptable. They taught me core values: honesty, integrity, keeping my word every single time, doing the right thing even when it's inconvenient or costs me money or might embarrass me. Those are the values I was taught. My dad lived those values every single day. He was a role model for me. He never took guff from anybody, because he had a strong sense of self and self-value.

Right before my dad died, he told me a story about when he was in the Navy during World War II. He was a country boy from Muskogee, Oklahoma. During the war in the Pacific, he was seaman first class, gunner on the ship, and the ship's boxer.

The captain walked by and said, "You son of a bitch," and my dad hit him. He didn't get thrown in the brig, because they were in the middle of a war. They were fighting every single day, and you couldn't give up your gunner, and they probably didn't want to give up the ship's boxer either. But he got busted from seaman first class to seaman second class.

"Nobody gets to disrespect my mama," he told me. His mother had died when he was eleven years old. He grew up with the utmost respect for his mother, and missed her. It didn't matter who said it: nobody got to call my dad a son of a bitch.

I didn't know that for a lot of years, and I admired that so much about him, that he would stand up to the authority in his world at the time and have boundaries. Who in your life has those kind of boundaries that won't accept disrespect? Is it your grandma? Maybe it's your kid that has such a strong sense of self. Maybe it's a boss that you've had in the past. Who in your life has been that kind of a person? Maybe it's a political leader. Think of Ronald Reagan when he stood in front of the world and said, "Mr. Gorbachev, tear down this wall."

I even have movie characters that I admire. I admire Rocky. Sylvester Stallone also gets some of my admiration, because when he wrote the movie *Rocky,* he was broke; I mean broke to the point of eating out of trash cans. He wrote a screenplay about a down-and-out boxer. They tried to buy that screenplay from him, but he had one condition: "I'll sell you the screenplay, but only if I get to play Rocky."

They wanted James Caan to play Rocky. They wanted Ryan O'Neal to play him. They had a whole list of actors they wanted to be Rocky. Nobody wanted Sylvester Stallone to play Rocky. But he held tight to his convictions, and he got to play Rocky in the movie. It changed his career. It changed a lot of people's lives, because of the strength that Rocky showed in the movie, his willingness to go the distance. If you've ever seen the movie, you know it's about going the distance. That's what he was all about. He went the distance and got that role.

So you can find role models in lots of different places. Right now, stop and identify who your role models are, and ask yourself, "Why is this person my role model? What attributes do they have in their life that I admire, that I would like to emulate in my own life?"

Take a few minutes right now. Get a sheet of paper if you have to, and identify your role models. Figure out why they are your role models, what attributes they have.

Once you've done that, let's talk about how you can develop those attributes. Let's talk about some simple things that might help you become the kind of person that other people will look up to and will someday put you on that list. Identify the attributes and start to develop them. Let's go through that now.

At this point you might be thinking, "This all sounds really good, but it's easy for Larry Winget to talk about this. It's not so easy for me. I'm struggling trying to find people to emulate. I'm struggling identifying the attributes that I want to live up to. I'm struggling with stepping into my full self because I'm afraid."

Listen, I have been there. I've always been Larry Winget, and I've always had that same set of core values, but I haven't always been the pit bull of personal development. When I first started out in this industry, I was pretty much your typical motivational speaker. I said what everybody said. I was a motivational speaker sheep; I went along with the herd. If it was a good idea to talk about positive attitude, I would talk about positive attitude, because everybody wanted to hear about positive attitude. All motivational speakers were talking about positive attitude, and audiences loved to hear about it. If I talked about setting goals, everybody loved that, because everybody talked about goal setting.

Only after years of being just like everybody else did I realize I was compromising my core values of honesty and authenticity by trying to be like everybody else instead of trying to be the best version of Larry Winget I could be.

I had to go through a transition. I had to go through letting go. I had to throw away all the things that were making me a living, and I had take a big risk. I had to be willing to say things that I knew would make people uncomfortable instead of comfortable, and see if I could still do it.

I was willing to go through that, and it was hard. I had to make a real transition in my life. I went away and holed up; I told my wife and my manager, "I don't know what's going to happen. I have to figure out who Larry Winget is."

One day I was watching Dennis Miller on television. He was talking in an interview about the Dennis Miller as he was at that time—being on *Saturday Night Live* as a comedian and doing sketch comedy. He was talking about how comedians go onstage to endear themselves to the audience so the audience will like them.

That's probably the way you are; certainly it was how I was. Dennis Miller said that comedians want people to like them because if they can get the audience to like them, they'll be more prone to laugh. He said, "The problem for me is that I'm not very endearing, so I gave it up."

The instant he said, "I'm not very endearing, so I gave it up," a light went on in my head. I realized that was my problem: I'm not very endearing either. So I decided to give it up. He said when he gave up that way of thinking, he became the Dennis Miller we all know him as today, the opinionated guy. That's when he got the NFL contract doing *Monday Night Football.* That's when he became a commentator on Fox News. That's when he got his own radio show.

When I was willing to let it all go and stop being endearing, it was a big risk for me, because I had to figure out whether anybody was going to pay me to do what I did. I had to figure if I was willing to risk it. I called my manager, I called my wife. I said, "I have no idea if this is going to work or not, but at least next time I go onstage, I'm going to be authentic. I'm going to say what I really believe. I'm going to give *my* speech instead of the audience's speech."

The next time I went onstage, I was heckled. A guy stood up and heckled me from the back of the room. It was a room of about 300 people. I listened to him, and the audience was embarrassed for him. I wheeled on him and said, "Buddy, you need to shut up, stop whining, and get a life." The audience jumped to their feet in a standing ovation.

I realized at that moment that that was a pretty good line: shut up, stop whining, and get a life. It was my gut reaction. This guy was playing a victim. I had no tolerance for victims. I still don't.

Because I was willing to put myself out there, speak my truth, and not avoid conflict, I was able to build on one line—shut up, stop whining, and get a life. I wrote a book by that title, which became a number-one *Wall Street Journal* best seller. I built the career I have today simply because I was willing to throw off trying to make everybody happy, trying to say only the words that made people feel good. I showed to myself and to my audiences that authenticity is the way to go. I was willing to say words that make people uncomfortable. I took the risk of saying words that might keep me from getting hired, but I discovered that people are so hungry for authenticity that they will pay a premium for it. I believe they'll pay a premium in your line of work too, regardless of what it is. I believe people seek authenticity more than any other thing.

I am convinced that people pay little attention to what you have to say. Most won't even believe what you have to say, but they will always pay attention to see if *you* believe what you have to say. You have to become a person who's willing to speak your truth, live your core values, and speak up for your core values in every situation. I promise you, you will be rewarded for it.

As we move forward, I'm going to give you some tips and techniques that you can use to develop the attributes of being the kind of person that you put on your list.

First thing, speak up. That means number one, don't mumble. Speak up, become articulate, use better words, use stronger words, stop using weak language. What is weak language? Saying, "You know, I think . . ." You think? Why don't you know? Too many people are thinking and not enough are knowing. I get tired of people saying, "Well, I think." I know it's what you think: the words are coming out of your mouth. Just tell me what you know. Just say what you mean.

Here's another one that bothers me—when people say, "In my humble opinion." Why is your opinion humble? I never say, "In my humble opinion," because my opinions are not humble. My opinions are my beliefs, and I have no humility about them. I believe strongly in them, and I am willing to speak up about them. What you're doing there is using a qualifier. Qualifiers always weaken speech.

Let me give you another one: "With all due respect." Then what follows is something that is totally disrespectful. People only say, "With all due respect" when they're getting ready to say something really rude. Why don't you just say, "I disagree"? That's much stronger, and much more truthful.

Stop compromising your beliefs. Stop using qualifiers and weak language.

Also stop apologizing. Why are you so sorry? People say, "I'm sorry" for so many things. Why are you sorry that you believe what you believe? "I'm sorry, but . . ." Why are you sorry? Why did you say that? What did you do wrong? You haven't done anything to me. You have nothing to apologize for. That's a qualifier. It's weak. Live boldly, speak boldly. Speak like you mean it.

The next part is the physical side. When I was a boy, every time I was going to do something, my dad would say, "Step lively." Speak boldly, but also walk boldly. In other words, walk with determination. Walk like you're going someplace. Don't lumber or meander along. Do what you do on purpose. Speak with purpose, walk with purpose.

Years ago, I was walking through New York City. It was the first time I had ever been to the big city. I was from Muskogee, Oklahoma, working for Southwestern Bell. The biggest city I'd probably been to was Dallas, maybe St. Louis, and I was in New York City, twenty-something, with another guy that was working with me on a project.

We were walking all over New York City, and we found ourselves in an area that I felt pretty good about. A cop walked up to me on the street and said, "You guys aren't from around here, and you need to go back to your part of town, down in Midtown, down around Times Square. You'll be OK there."

I said, "Aren't we OK here?"

"No, you're not OK walking along here."

I looked up, and there was a little old lady up ahead of us walking along. I said, "Well, she's all by herself, and she's walking along, and she's just fine."

The cop said to me something I've never forgotten. He said, "She looks like she knows where she's going. No one will bother her. You guys don't look like you know where you're going. You're about to be victims."

I said, "Oh, OK. I get it. Thank you." We got in a cab and went back to Midtown. Went back down to Times Square, where the tourists were.

Are you walking through life like a tourist? Do you look as if you know where you're going? Do you walk with purpose? Do you carry yourself with purpose? Do you speak with purpose because you're confident in the words that come out of your mouth? If you're always trying to catch your language saying, "Will this offend anyone? Will this make everyone happy?

How can I word this so no one will get their feelings hurt?" Then you're never going to speak with purpose.

Speak your truth. Speak up for yourself. Speak up for what is right, and speak up about what is wrong. Don't hesitate to do that. Be a person who has clear values, and speak up for those values. If people don't like it, tough. You have now become a person who has risen above the approval of others. By learning to speak up, by using better language so you will no longer speak with weak language, and by carrying yourself with purpose, you will change how others respond to you, and you will start to be more successful.

Next, be honest. We've always heard that honesty is the best policy. No: honesty is the *only* policy. Tell the truth no matter what. If you've done something wrong, tell the truth about it. In a job situation, a good boss would rather have an employee that admits they've made a mistake, takes responsibility for it, and says, "I did this. I'm sorry." They're willing to apologize, and they have a plan for fixing the problem. Good bosses will respect that, but they don't respect somebody who tries to duck responsibility and is less than honest about whose fault it was.

If you've made a mistake, admit it. It's about taking responsibility, and that comes down to always being honest. Teach your kids to be honest in every situation. Honesty, as I've already said, is my number-one principle. It will always be rewarded in the long run.

That also goes hand-in-hand with excuses. Don't make excuses. Benjamin Franklin said, "If you're good at making excuses, you're seldom good for anything else." I like that. Don't make excuses. Just take responsibility.

Don't whine. For some people, whining is their best friend. We have become a nation of whiners, where we complain about everything.

My son was in the 82nd Airborne Division. He had a tour of duty in Iraq. He was in Bosnia, and he had a buddy who was with him through all that. My son got out and came back and became a cop, but this guy stayed in the Army and became a helicopter pilot. This week his Facebook post said: "My room here in Afghanistan is six foot by eight foot. That is exactly the size of a prison cell in America. I eat meat every day that is also served in prisons. I know because it says so on the box. I will be leaving Afghanistan in forty days to come back to your world, and I read every morning on Facebook about how my latte wasn't hot enough today, how it's raining, and the traffic is going to be slower today, how I had a flat tire, and now my day is ruined." He said, "I hope I can figure out how to make it in your world."

We whine about First World problems. We whine about things that make no difference in the long run. We've lost perspective, so we whine about everything. Most of what we complain about, we won't even remember two hours from now, maybe not two minutes from now.

Get over it. There's a time to speak up, and there is a time to shut up. Most of what we gripe about doesn't matter. Get over it. Get over yourself and move on.

Next is this. Learn to walk away. Let me tell you what I mean by that. You have friends you need to walk away from; we've already talked about that. You have situations you need to walk away from. I am big on speaking up. I am big on confrontation if something is wrong, but I also know we all reach the point where nothing we say and nothing we do is going to make any difference. Walk away. Just leave it.

I learned years ago that if I was going to ever step up in my career, I was going to have to learn to step away from a given situation. I wrote this little line that described my feelings and what I learned from that experience: *you can't step up to the next level as long as you keep one foot on the lower level.* Many of you right now are keeping your foot on the lower level of life because you're not willing to let go of that level. You say you want to step up. Those are just words until you take your foot off the level you're on right now and step full-on to the one where you want to be.

Next is this: make some plans. In my book *Grow a Pair,* I called them big, bold, brash, ballsy plans. Many motivational bozos out there will talk to you about the power of goal setting. That's fine. But I'm not big on setting goals. I'm big on making plans. Plans are different than goals. Goals, to me, especially because of how we've treated them in the last few years, are not much more than New Year's resolutions. We say, "I want to be a millionaire." Well, what's your plan for getting there? "I don't have a plan. I just want to be a millionaire, and I've been told if you speak it, you can claim it. Whatever you believe, you can achieve."

No. That's not true. Whatever you have a plan for, and you get up every morning and go to work on, you will increase your likelihood of achieving, but there's no guarantee you will achieve it. You certainly don't achieve it by creating a dream board and putting up pictures of the Maserati you want to drive.

This might hurt your feelings, because you live and die by your little dream board. You put little motivational sayings up every day, and you speak them every morning, thinking that is going to change your life. You write down your list of 100 things you want to achieve, and you carry it around with you. Basically, those are dreams.

Here's the reality. Jiminy Cricket lied to you. Dreams don't come true. Those are weak words.

They were told to you by people who were trying to sell you an idea that has nothing to do with real achievement, which is always based on work. You don't believe your way to success; you work your way to success.

A plan is much different than a dream. A plan is much different than a goal. A plan has doable parts— things that I can do today that move me from where I am so I can do more tomorrow.

Too many people are setting goals, and they don't have any plans. Even when they make plans, they don't make a big, challenging plans. If I have a plan tomorrow to get to the cleaners, that's not very challenging.

You may be driving around right now with clothes in the back seat of your car. You've been driving around with them for a week, and you didn't get to the cleaners, so you didn't even achieve that plan. You know why you didn't? It wasn't a priority. It wasn't important to you. If it had been important to you, you would have gotten it done.

Write a plan for a project, something you want to have happen in your life that is truly important to you, something you can make a priority, something that drives you, something that excites you, something that you can get determined about.

The problem is we don't make those kind of plans. We make silly, little, weak plans about which that we never have to do anything because we know there's no consequence if we don't achieve them. What's so earth-shattering if you didn't get to the dry cleaners? You won't have a clean shirt on Monday. That's not a good thing, but there's no real consequence.

I like to make plans that have consequences, so there's a penalty for nonperformance when I don't carry them out. I like plans that challenge me to be my best every single day. I like plans where I know there's something I can do about them today. That's what a real plan is.

I'm not like the motivational folks, telling you to have dreams. I'm not telling you to create one of those silly dream boards. I'm not even telling you to set goals. Way too many people are into goal setting, and not enough of them are into goal achievement. I'm talking about creating a plan with doable action steps that you can actually get up tomorrow and go to work on. That's what will make things happen in your life. That's what will create the kind of results that up until now you've just been saying you want.

Here's another one. Learn to walk up to people, look them in the eye, and shake their hand. That sounds so trite. That sounds so ridiculous. But think about it. How many people will look you in the eye and shake your hand? I mean a real handshake, not that weak-fish thing.

Does that really matter? It absolutely matters. I judge whether I want to do business with a person based on how they shake my hand and whether they can look me in the eye or not. If you can't look me in the eye and shake my hand, we probably will never have any kind of a relationship at all.

Is that fair? It doesn't have to be fair. It's what I believe. It doesn't have to be fair. It just has to be right for me. You may say, "Larry, I think you're wrong." OK, it can be wrong for you, but for me, you'd better be able to look me in the eye.

One of the very first things my dad taught me— when I was a little, bitty boy, three years old—was that when I met someone, I should look him in the eye, stick my hand out, and say, "Hello, my name is Larry Winget."

I have grandsons right now that I'm working on. I want them to be able to stick their hands out, look somebody in the eye, shake their hand, and say, "Hello, my name is . . ." That's an important attribute; it will say a lot about you. You need to be able to do that.

Here's another one. I want you to learn to say "no more." Chances are, you've been saying yes to way too many things. You end up doing things you don't want to do and don't like to do simply because you don't have the guts to say no to them.

Let me give you an example. I don't eat out with people I don't like. I just don't. I won't go to lunch with them. I don't do lunch meetings. I don't do din-ner if I do an after-dinner speech. I only eat with people I enjoy. That's it. Very simple. I want to enjoy the person I'm having lunch with, breaking bread with. That's selfish, it's hedonistic, but I'll guarantee you I'm a better person for it.

I don't go to movies I don't want to see. I don't hang around people I don't want to be around. I don't do things I don't want to do. Does that mean that I don't see the movies my wife wants to see? Yeah, it does. It means I'll say, "I don't want to see that one. Why don't you find a friend, or why don't you go when I'm on the road?" I'm on the road a lot.

She says, "I get it." After being together as long as we have, I don't ask her to participate in things she doesn't enjoy, but when we do things together, we both enjoy them and have a lot of fun doing them. When we go out to eat with people, they're people we like being with.

You can waste my money, and I'll be mad about it. You waste my time, and I'm upset about it, because time is that important to me. I protect my time. Are you protecting yours, or are you saying yes? Have you become a doormat to people who come to you every single time, because they know you'll always say yes? Learn to say no more.

I recently wrote a blog with my five friends. We were talking about what we've learned over all our years that we wish we had learned much earlier to make ourselves happier and more successful. To a man, we all said we wish we had learned to say no a whole lot earlier. So if you want to be more successful, if you want to be happier, if you want to be the kind of person we're talking about here, learn to say no.

Here's one more. Have clear priorities. People talk about time management. You don't need time management. You need priority management. If it matters to you, you will do it.

If you don't know what your priorities are, I do. Let me walk through your house. Let me look at your closet. Let me look at your credit-card statement. Let me look at your bank statement. I can tell you what your priorities are simply because your time, your energy, and your money always go to what's important to you. That's it. Your time, your energy, and your money always go to what's important to you, not what you say is important to you. They go to what's really important to you.

People tell me it's important for them to be financially secure, but they have no money in savings, so it's not important for them. What's really important to them is to drive a car that impresses other people, to have a big-screen TV hanging on their wall, to have a closet full of clothes that they've just bought at the mall. How do I know? I look at their money.

Their money went to what was really important to them, not to what they said was important.

Look at your life. Track your money. Understand what your priorities are. Then I want you to get better priorities. I want you to get clear about what really matters to you. When you start living your life not for the approval of others but by priorities based on what is important to you in the long term, that's when you'll start to be successful.

I've been giving you lots of ideas here, and you may be still pushing back. You may be saying, "Larry, I'm not that kind of a person. I'm an introvert. I'm shy. I'm not the kind of person who speaks up or says no. I can't tell people exactly what I think. I just can't be that way."

I understand that some people's personalities make them shy. Some people truly are introverts. I get that. That's still not an excuse for you to shy away from your core beliefs and your core values. It's still not a reason that you can compromise what you believe in just to get along.

You can be introverted and strong. You can be shy and still really firm in your core beliefs and your core values. You can be shy and introverted and all of those other things, and still have clear priorities. You can know the difference between right and wrong in your life and stand up for that.

I get that not everybody can be as loud and assertive as I am, but still I can show you people who are shy and introverted, who have a set of core values that they will never compromise; everybody knows what they believe. Being shy or introverted is not an excuse for you to compromise. Don't ever think it is.

You have to find the style that works best for you. I understand there is a difference in styles, so please be assured that you can be a shy person, you can be an introverted person, and you can still be a person who is politically incorrect.

These are some specific steps that you can take in order to achieve more, do more, have more in your life, and to become a person who has clear priorities and values, and knows how to speak up and live them in every area of life. Next we're going to discuss how you can use these steps in your career and in your business.

3
The Power of Responsibility

I want to begin with my number-one rule for both life and business: *do what you said you would do when you said you would do it, the way you said you would do it.*

That is my number-one rule. Why is that so important? Because that's all anybody wants. Think about your life. All your spouse wants from you is for you to do what you said you would do when you said you would do it, the way you said you would do it. All your kids want from you as a parent is for you to do what you said you would do when you said you would do it, the way you said you would do it. That's all you want from your kids as well. That's all we want from our friends. That's what we want from everybody we come in contact with.

Let's move it over to your business. That's all you want from your employers. You want them to do what they said they would do. You want them to do what they said they would do when you hired them. That's all we're looking for.

That's exactly what a customer wants from you as well, whether you're an entrepreneur, a solopreneur, or a Fortune 500 corporation. Customers want the business they do business with, the company they share their money with, to do what they said they would do when they said they would do it, the way they said they would do it. Don't we want the same things from our customers? Don't we want them to pay when they said they would the way they said they would?

That's why that rule is so all-encompassing. It applies to everything in both our personal life and in our business life. It is a very simple rule to live your life and run your business by. It will make your customers happy, your employees happy, your employer happy. It'll make your family work much better.

Keep that rule in mind when you wake up in the morning. Keep it in mind as you go to work every single day. That rule is based in integrity. It means we're keeping our word. It's based in honesty. It's based in doing the right thing. It's based in work. It's based in authenticity.

My core values are reflected in that rule, and those core values will work for you just as well, because that rule will keep you honest. It will make sure that you're living a life and running a business based in integrity. It will make sure that you're providing excellent customer service and adding value to the customer experience. It'll make sure you're a good leader and a good boss. It'll make sure you're a good employee.

When people don't live by this rule in running their life and their business, they have problems. In fact, this rule addresses most of the core challenges in business today.

The first challenge is going to be from an entitled and unskilled workforce. Now this is going to make a lot of you millennials mad, but I'm going to focus now the eighteen- to thirty-four-year-olds. People in this age group typically have a more entitled mentality. Whose fault is that?

Believe it or not, I don't blame the millennials. I blame their boomer parents, who didn't do a good job. I wrote a best-selling book called *Your Kids Are Your Own Fault*. That is a politically incorrect title, because when you start saying *fault*, people automatically think that you're blaming them.

But *fault* just means *consequence*. Your actions cause a consequence. If I'm rich, that's my fault. If I'm healthy, that's my fault. If I'm stupid, that's my fault. If I'm broke, that's my fault. Fault is associated with consequences, and your kids are the result of your actions. The millennials feel entitled right now because we, the boomers, didn't do a good job of teaching them work ethic and responsibility. Nor are we doing a good job of teaching them personal responsibility and a strong work ethic.

Right now in America, 60 percent of adults are financially supporting their adult children, the millennials, in some way. Parents aren't forcing independence. That's wrong. When you have an increasing number of adult children who are moving back in with their parents, that's a problem.

I believe parenting has one goal, and that's independence. You raise your kids so they will go away. You've given them the skills to be able to stand on their own two feet and be self-reliant. If your adult children are still dependent on you, let me make one of those politically incorrect statements: you were a lousy parent, because you didn't make sure that your children had the skills to go away and survive and thrive in the real world. If they are living with you now, you are enabling them by allowing them to be dependent on you.

If we're going to survive as we move forward in business, we need for boomers, adult parents, to step up and be real parents to their children. And their adult children, the millennials, are at some point going to have to take responsibility for their lives, become self-reliant and independent, and learn how to survive and thrive on their own.

Of course there are boomers who will say, "I was a great parent." OK, good. Then I'm not talking about you. There are millennials who are very successful and are great entrepreneurs, great employees. They're becoming wonderful employers and great solopreneurs and are achieving great things. If your kids are like that, I'm not talking to you right now. I'm talking to the others. Their kids are not doing well, and that is the challenge.

A recent study by a Princeton research group said that by comparison to their counterparts in nearly thirty other countries, American millennials ranked dead last in the world in terms of skill sets— meaning everyone was ahead of them in literacy and in basic math skills. That's a problem, folks. If you can't read, and you can't add and subtract, chances are you're not going to do well in business.

We have role models out there right now that brag about the fact they don't read books. Kanye West was recently reported as saying, "I don't read books. They're full of arrogance." Again, I don't let people by with that stupidity. I call people on that stuff. You cannot survive, you cannot be successful if you're not reading books. But most people don't read. We have bookstores, but most people go to bookstores these days for a cup of coffee, not to read a book. It's sad too when you realize that the average American will never read a nonfiction book after high school. You have to be able to read, and when we rank dead last in literacy on the world level, on the global scene, that's a problem, also when we can't do basic math.

The other area where millennials ranked dead last is that they don't have the ability to follow directions. They don't even have the computer skills to be able to survive in the workplace.

People will say I'm making a generalization about millennials. Folks, these are not generalizations. They are facts from a study. If you're a millennial, and you don't like this, and it doesn't apply to you, you ought to be upset enough to help the people within your generation start to do better so it doesn't apply to them as well. But don't be surprised when American businesses have to go outside the United States for talent, because that's what's going to happen when our talent pool is not deep enough here for businesses to do well in the future.

I don't like the statistics that happen to apply to my generation. I hate the fact that two-thirds of boomers are not in any way prepared for retirement and that consequently, when they retire, somebody's going to be taking care of them. That means those of us who pay taxes will be supporting them, because they didn't plan well enough to support themselves. I don't like that.

Does it make it any less true because I don't like it? No. It's still true. It's a fact I can't argue with, so I will do what I can to help people become more financially literate, to help them save, and to change that percentage for the individuals who are willing to learn.

That is the job of millennials. That is the job of boomers: to help people step up. But in the next ten years or so, American businesses are going to be primarily full of millennials in the workforce, and their skill levels aren't up to where they need to be.

We were told that education was about the three R's—writing, reading, and 'rithmetic. I need to add two more: *responsibility* and *respect*. We have to be teaching those things because a lack of those five R's will result in the downfall of American business because we simply don't respect our customers enough to serve them well, don't respect management enough to do our job, don't take personal responsibility for our actions, and want to blame others. We don't have basic literacy or math skills, and we can't articulate ourselves in writing well enough to do well in the business world. If that doesn't scare you, there's something wrong with you. If we're going to be successful moving forward, we have to get back to those things.

Let me tell you another area that I'm concerned about in American business today: we don't serve our customers well. Customers are interested in value, and they will go wherever they find value. If they are going to shop on price alone, don't be surprised that the big-box stores do so well, because they can buy in such great volume that if people are shopping price alone, that's where they will get the best price.

Differentiation, understanding what sets you apart and how you can become unique, is what will keep you from becoming a commodity. A commodity is something you shop for based on price. You don't want to compete based on price, because somebody can always be a nickel cheaper. That means you're going to have to step up your game in serving your customers. You're going to have to be the kind of person who always does what they said they would do when they said they would do it, the way they said they would do it.

Now here's the good news for those of us who are entrepreneurs and solopreneurs today: it takes less than it ever has before. It's sad, but that's good news for us. Learning how to say "please" and "thank you," learning how to appreciate customers as individuals, learning how to go back to basics and look them in the eye, telling them you appreciate their business—I don't get that from online shopping; I don't get that from the big-box stores, who have to hire minimum-wage people in order to survive. I'm not a price shopper. I'm a service shopper, I'm a value shopper, so I'll pay more for that experience.

In the future, it's going to be more about creating the right customer experience. That will always come down to one-on-one human connection. You must get good at that.

We're also going to have to learn to speak up when we don't get good customer service. Things change when we become uncomfortable. So if you are in business and someone speaks up and tells you you're not serving them well, instead of getting mad, I suggest that you thank that person for pointing it out, because becoming uncomfortable about the service that you have provided will allow you the opportunity to improve. It will enable you to improve how you do things and the way you serve your customers. You will get better, and you will make more customers happy. Customer service, adding value, getting more for less, increasing the level of customer experience, creating a uniqueness—that's what will help us move forward.

The next area of concern for me is the quality of our leadership. Unfortunately, leadership is not a talent we admire as much as we once did. We feel we can criticize our boss instead of respecting him or her. Now you may say bosses aren't as respectable as they once were. I'm with you there. Believe me, I will not argue.

The qualities I mentioned earlier, the attributes that we created in that list of people you admire and why you admire them—I'll bet you those are the qualities that you want in a leader. You want honesty. You want a leader to speak up. You want an honest leader who will speak up and say, "This is right. This is wrong. This is what we believe in. This is who we are. This is what we are about. These are our core values."

It's a shame that people who don't have those qualities have been elevated to places of leadership. We're going to have to require more from our leadership. We're going to have to be better leaders in order to attract the followers who will help us accomplish what we need to do.

We don't value the right things right now. We admire the wrong things. We need to get back to valuing what's really important: honesty, integrity, doing the right things, having core values. This may sound to you like common sense, and it is, but as you know, common sense is no longer common.

These ideas sound simple, but they are complicated to pull off, because we have let things slide for too long. We accept bad service and don't speak up. We let lousy leaders get by. Leaders let lousy employees slide.

If we're going to retain market share, if we're going to grow and be successful in running our businesses, we have to stand up for adding value for our customers; we're going to have to stand up to our employees and for our employees. We have to become the kind of business that others want to share their money with; we have to have the skills necessary for serving our customers, our company, and our country well. That means we have to be able to respect each other, be responsible for our behavior, and do the basics, like follow directions, write, read, add, and subtract.

At this point you may be saying, "Larry, I'm with you. I'm willing to do all of those things, but I can't find employment. I have to live with mommy and daddy. I have to take government assistance. I can't find the kind of career I am looking for."

Here's my advice. If you're unemployed, stop looking for a career and get a job. There's a big difference between finding a career and accepting a job, and there's no shame in working at something you don't like if it pays the bills.

We've reached a point in society where we think that we have to love everything we do. No. There's a line that has been with us for many years: *as long as you love what you do, you'll never work a day in your life.* You've heard that; I've heard that. It's a load of crap, because if you are really working, there's going to be a whole lot about it you don't love. I don't care how much you love it, if you're doing it well and doing it consistently, there will be parts of it that you're going to hate. That's the reality of work. That's what we need to understand.

You can't love what you do every single day. Stop trying to find a career and follow your passion and figure out a way to pay your bills. Right now people don't care as much about paying their bills and keeping their word as they once did. We lack a commitment to our commitments.

I am committed to paying my bills, my obligations. You may be saying, "I have a house payment. I have a car payment. I have utilities." Those are your obligations. You made a commitment to pay those people, and if you honor those commitments, you'll do whatever it takes to make sure that you keep them. This means that you'll get your dreams and your ego out of the way and take a job, because keeping your commitments is important to you.

If you're unemployed, find a job. You know the best way to find a career? By having a job. Many people are saying, "I don't love what I do. I want to find another job," and they quit. That's dumb. Never quit the job you have to find a job you love. Keep the job you have, no matter how much you hate it. I don't know about you, but I've come to like having money in my pocket. I like it when my creditors don't call me. I like being able to pay my bills. That's what's most important to me. Keep the job you have so you can do those things while you are in search of the job you want.

It's OK to hate your job while you are in search of the job of your dreams, the job that will fulfill you, the job that will create passion and purpose and all of that. But keep a commitment to your commitments, and honor the fact that you have a job by honoring your employer, by doing the work you were hired to do.

Many people say, "I am underemployed." Get over it. After I left AT&T and Southwestern Bell, I started my own telecommunications company, and I went to work one day. The corporation commission ruled that what I did was no longer going to be legal, and they didn't grandfather me in. One day I went to work the president of the company, doing really well, and I went home out of business. I'd lost everything.

I asked my neighbors if I could mow their yards and rake their leaves. Was that humiliating? Yes, it was humiliating. Why did I do it? I had a commitment to my commitments. I had kids. I had people who relied on me, so I set my ego aside and earned money. Did I like it? No. I hated it, but I did what it took.

If you are really committed to becoming successful, you will do whatever it takes. There is great honor in having a job, even a job you don't like, when you give it all you have and when you have earned the money you receive.

So if you're underemployed, get over yourself until you can find a job where you can earn the kind of money that is commensurate with your education and your background. By the way, don't be surprised when you get a degree in basket weaving and no one will hire you as a computer programmer. What are you thinking? There's not a big demand for basket weavers.

Do you know you can get a bachelor's degree in puppetry? Excuse me? Unless *Sesame Street* is hiring or the Muppets are looking for a new hand to go inside Oscar the Grouch, chances are you're going to be unemployed, and you'll be a barista somewhere.

So when you are parents helping your kids make decisions for their life, do them a favor. Guide them into areas that will be marketable, that they can get paid for in the future.

Again I'm going to go back to the millennials: according to a recent study, 60 percent of them said they had no intention of going into business, and 48 percent said they had never been encouraged to do so.

At this point it's not the failure of the millennials. It's a failure of the parents and our school systems, because they are not preparing people for survival in a business climate. They're not preparing them for how to get a job and work. We have too many people who are being encouraged to follow their dreams and find their passion. Then they are surprised when they don't have any job skills that are marketable, and they can't make a six-figure income when they have a $10-an-hour education.

All right. You have a job. You want to do well in the job. You're an employee. Let me talk to you about what it takes to be a successful employee and what you need to remember.

First of all, you need to remember you're paid to work. You're not paid to make personal calls. You're not paid to come in late. You're not paid to follow social media or any other personal activity. That is not your right as an employee. You were hired to work. You were told what the job was when you agreed to take it. That's what you're paid to do.

Many people tell me, "Yeah, but that's something I ought to be able to do. It's my time. I'm not doing anything right now. I don't have a customer in front of me. I ought to be able to text my friends." No, you're not paid to do that, and if you're not paid to do it, you shouldn't be doing it.

You also need to remember this if you're an employee: you're just an expense. Sorry to devalue you, but you need to understand that if the cost to have you employed exceeds your value as an employee, there is no reason for the company to employ you.

It's really that simple. If it costs more to have you than you're worth to the company, there's no reason for them to employ you. So your goal as an employee is to always be adding value. People tell me, "I'd like to make more money." Why don't you be *worth* more money?

The first thing you can do is add value to the workplace, and you will be rewarded for it. Now somebody always wants to say, "No, Larry, I tried that. It didn't work out for me." I recently talked about this in my own social media, and someone said, "Yeah, I hope that works out for you."

This is victim mentality. The way it works is that you are always rewarded for the service you provide. If you provide more service, in other words put more work into your hour, then you will be paid more for that hour. It's a universal principle that can't be denied. There will be exceptions, but I'm talking about this as a universal principle. That's how it works. Understand that you're an expense, and always add value.

Furthermore, no one likes a whiner, or a complainer, or a troublemaker, or a gossip. If you're an employee, you're not paid to whine or complain or gossip or be a troublemaker, but I'll tell you what everybody *does* like. Every boss, manager, leader adores this kind of person. It's the kind of person who will do what it takes to get the job done, who is willing to be of service to anyone, who can be counted on every single time. Be that employee.

You also need to remember that businesses don't exist to make their employees happy. Businesses exist for one reason and one reason only, and that's to be profitable. They become profitable by serving customers well, and you need to be a part of that process.

All employers want their employees to be happy, but that's not why they exist. If you go to work expecting that your boss and your company are there to make sure you have a good day every single day and keep your feelings from being hurt by your stupid coworkers, it's just not true.

The employer *is* legally obligated to create a safe working environment, where nothing falls on your head and you don't get hurt. That's about it, folks. You need to face that. They don't exist to make you happy.

Your job is not to whine, but to be the kind of person others can count on, to do what you're paid to do, to make sure that your value exceeds your cost, and to understand you are there to help the company be more profitable. That's it.

I'm a hard-ass about this stuff. I've run companies. People who say they have a stupid boss or work for a stupid company ought to try running one. It's a challenge. You try starting your own company, you try running one, you try keeping one profitable, and you'll sing a different tune.

Let's move on to employers. I'm not just hard on employees; I'm hard on employers too. I have big expectations for people who hire people and expect to get the best from them.

Here's my number-one thing for employers to know: if you have lousy employees, it's because you are a lousy employer. If you have stupid employees, you were a stupid manager for hiring them. You didn't do a good job, because your employees are going to be no better than you are.

This goes back to the very first principle of this book. Do you remember it? *Fix yourself first.* Don't think you can be a leader or an effective manager and go in and try to fix all of your employees. You must fix yourself first.

If you have employees who are showing up late, are you showing up late? If you have employees who are disrespectful, are you disrespectful? Your employees have the same relationship with you as kids do with their parents. They will mirror you. They will reflect you. So don't talk bad about your employees. It's *you* you're talking about.

Moreover, your job as a boss is to make your company the best place for a customer to do business with. That means you have to hire the best people, and you have to give them the best training.

You have to be the best example for your employees to emulate, and you have to drive home the concept of value with every single person who works there. Everyone from the janitor on up needs to understand that they contribute to overall customer satisfaction. They need to see their role in that process, so they will help serve the customer well.

Sometimes the people in the back don't understand that they are just as much a part of serving the customer, just as much a part of bringing value to the customer, as the people who have face-to-face or voice-to-voice interaction with a customer. Your job as a manager is to explain that everyone's role is to add value to the customer.

Your next job as an employer is to stand up for what's right. I don't want you to even think about whether this is the easiest thing to do or the cheapest thing to do or the fastest thing to do, because sometimes the right thing to do is the hardest, and it's the most expensive, and it's the slowest thing you can do. However, the right thing is the right thing regardless. Always do the right thing.

Next, remember that your employees they can't read your mind. Don't expect them to know what you want if you haven't communicated that to them and taught them how to do it. Your role as an employer is to determine what you want from people, hire well, communicate what you want, teach them how to give you what you want, impose consequences when you don't get what you want, and give rewards when you do.

See how simple that is! Go through that basic process, and you'll be a better manager.

Also, hire slow, and fire fast. Most employers have that one backwards: they hire fast and fire slow. Then they wonder why they don't have the respect of their employees. It's because they have tolerated bad employees, and their bad work habits have infected the rest of the workforce. The workforce will lose respect for you as a manager because you didn't do what they all know you should have done, which was fire that bad employee.

You will spend a lot less time firing, though, if you do a good job of hiring. Make sure to hire people who can and are willing to get the job done. It all comes down to two things: willingness and ability. I can teach anyone the ability to do almost anything. I can't teach willingness. Hire for willingness, and then teach them the ability.

Finally, if you put up with it, you're endorsing it. So let me ask you this as an employer. Do you endorse being late? Being late, by the way, is rude. Do you endorse rudeness? Do you endorse lack of respect? Then why are you putting up with it?

Do you endorse disrespect to your customers? Then why are you putting up with it? Do you endorse people getting paid for something they aren't doing? Then why are you putting up with it?

It's hard to be a manager. There's a reason you get paid more than employees. It's because you have to work harder and do more than employees. More is expected from you. Employers need to step it up.

Let's talk about another aspect of business: teamwork. Now I'm going to upset a lot of you, because I'm not a big supporter of teamwork. I think *teamwork* is a word a lot like *passion*. It sounds good but doesn't mean much. It's become nothing more than a buzzword. "Oh, we have to be team players." I'm not looking for team players. I'm looking for people who can get stuff done.

Teamwork doesn't work. That's a bold statement, and I'll guarantee you that's politically incorrect, and right now you may be spewing coffee out of your nose, because you love your team. For you, it's all about your team. Sorry, I'm right. You're wrong.

Teamwork doesn't work, and here's why. Someone on the team isn't going to work, which means that the team didn't do the work. It means that it was a handful of superstar employees got together and accomplished the job, and not the team, because there's always some bozo over there in the corner who did not do one darn thing to make it happen. You know what I'm talking about. You have people on your team right now who don't do anything, yet when the team gets rewarded, they are right there to help share that credit, aren't they?

If you're a superstar—and I hope you are—you know the people who are not contributing. Superstars don't worry about the team. They respect the other superstars who will support them in achieving a common goal.

You'll say that's not how it works in sports. Yes, it's exactly how it works in sports. The goal is to win the game. Superstars look to each other for support in making sure that happens. Do they have to work together? Yes, but that's not called teamwork. That is superstar employees working together and being able to count on the talents of others they know will show up and do their part.

That's a big difference. A superstar will show up and do their part. It doesn't have to be the quarterback. It doesn't have to be the lead point scorer, or the super salesperson. A superstar employee might be the janitor. Yep—the superstar employee might be the janitor, because that's a person who can be counted on to do their job. It's a very important job. You don't believe it? Take a look at all the full trash cans and dirty restrooms and filthy floors. Would that work in your business? I wouldn't like it in my business. It wouldn't work. If it didn't get done, would there be a big hole left in the overall performance? Yes. So the janitor is a critical player.

A superstar can be counted on to do their part, regardless of what their job title is, regardless of what their role is. It's a person who contributes and whose presence would be missed. But there are people on your team who, if they didn't show up for work tomorrow, wouldn't be missed, because they don't contribute.

So teamwork is really about superstar employees, regardless of what their job title is, showing up and doing their part to contribute where they would be missed if they weren't there. It's about people who are dedicated to excellence and making sure that the common goal of the company is achieved.

Now let's talk about going into business for yourself, becoming an entrepreneur, maybe a solopreneur. The question that's often asked is, are entrepreneurs born, or are they made? The answer to that is very simple. Yes.

Some people really are born to be entrepreneurs. They are ready to go into business all on their own. They're figuring out a way to make money in as many different ways as possible. They're ready to open up their first lemonade stand. They're ready to pick up cans on the side of the road. They're ready to do whatever it takes to earn money. They are ready to be in business.

These people don't work well with others. They aren't team players. (Some people count that as a negative, but you know how I feel about teamwork.) I admire people who are that way. I was good at working in a corporation, but I was really good at working for myself. I discovered over the years that I was the best boss I ever had, but I was also the worst boss I ever had.

Can an entrepreneur be born? Absolutely. Does that ensure that an entrepreneur will be successful? Absolutely not. Entrepreneurs may be born to work for themselves and to run and create a business, but that does not mean that they will be successful. Most entrepreneurs, 95 percent of the people who go into business on their own, are going to fail in the first five years. You've heard that statistic. Why is that?

Let's look quickly at why businesses fail. First of all, I believe that businesses fail because people have no preparation. They just don't know what they're doing.

These days people talk about going into business for themselves, and there are a lot of multilevel marketing (MLM) companies out there. There are a lot of ways to get into companies on the Internet who market through Facebook and so forth, and that sounds so appealing. I am not putting those companies down, because somebody's making money. But before you jump into a company like that, do your research, and be prepared. Find out how many of the people in that organization are making money. Know what the failure rate is. Know what the pay-back time is.

You know, you have to buy in. When do you get your money back? How long does it typically take? What are the averages? How many people have entered into that MLM business? How many of the people who entered it five years ago are still doing it now? I want to know what the turnover rate is. I want you to ask those questions of the company you're signing up with. If they don't have the answers, walk away. I don't care how good it sounds to you or how much they tease you with all of the money you can make.

Believe me, I've heard the promises. The promises are huge, but you need to know this: as soon as you run through your circle of friends, you're done. That's how those businesses work. What are you going to do then? Do you know? Do you have a plan, or are you following a dream? Or do you just hate your job so much that you think this is the way to escape the drudgery and get to be your own boss?

Most people should not become their own boss, because they don't have the discipline and the work ethic to be good at it. They find it too easy to sit around in their pajamas, watch the morning shows, and drink coffee. Finally, around 11:00, they'll get up and start to do something. They'll get on the phone for a little while, and they'll receive a little bit of rejection, and they'll say, "Today's not my day. I'll do it tomorrow."

That's not how you become successful. You do it whether it's your day or not. You do it whether you get rejection or not. You don't have the luxury of sitting around in your pajamas until 11:00 before you start. That's not how it works.

Chances are, you have no business of becoming your own boss. You need a job. Keep your job, but if you do decide to go into business, you need to be prepared. If you're interested in an MLM company, ask those tough questions. If you're going to start your own company, you need to answer these questions too.

The first question is, do you have real-world, hands-on experience in running a business, or have you just talked yourself into the idea you can do it? Which one is it? It's one or the other. Do you have real-world experience?

I watch a lot of business shows on television. One has to do with restaurant startups. It's always interesting to me when the guys on the show talk to people who have decided to start their own restaurant, and they ask what their experience is. Many people have convinced themselves that their food is so good, or that they have such a passion for it, that they will be successful, yet they have no experience.

Or someone will have been a waiter. "I was a waiter in three restaurants while I was going to college, and I can really cook a pizza, so I know I can run a successful restaurant." The people on this show are very clear: before we invest money in you, we want to see your business plan, because we're not buying your passion. We're not buying your drive. We can find people with passion and drive every single day, but if they don't have the skills, if they don't have the commitment, and they don't have a business plan, there's no reason to invest in them.

You may sit back and say, "Well, I wouldn't invest in them anyway." But if you don't have the same skills, if all you have is passion and drive, why would you invest in yourself? You can't talk yourself into the idea that you have experience. You need real-world experience. Go out and work for somebody, learn from them, watch what they do right, watch what they do wrong, and put together a plan to do better when you start your own company, if that's your choice.

Next let me ask you this. Have you ever read a book on how to start or run a business? There are lots of books. You can go online and order books about how to do just about anything in the whole world. You should do that.

I have people who come to me and say, "My business is not doing very well."

The first thing I say is, "How many books did you read before you went into business?"

"I didn't read anything."

Why not? All the information you need is available, I promise you. All you have to do is go to any search engine and type in, "How do I . . ." and then type out whatever it is you want to know. You can probably go on YouTube and say, "How do I . . ." and there will be a YouTube teaching you how to do it.

No matter what you want to do, somebody else has done it. They've probably written a book, and you can learn from that book. You have to go out and take advantage of the knowledge that other people have put down on paper, or maybe recorded on a YouTube video. If you don't do that, sorry: you're too stupid to go into business for yourself. Don't be surprised when you fail.

Here's another question. Have you taken a course on marketing or advertising? Because I don't care how good your product is, if you can't sell it, it ain't happening. That's what it comes down to.

The dumbest thing ever taught is this line: "Build a better mousetrap, and the world will beat a path to your door." It's an old line; believe me, I know; my mama and daddy used to tell it to me. But it's stupid.

We have lots of people with amazing products who can't figure out how to stay in business. You have your favorite restaurants over the years that have probably gone out of business because they didn't know how to be in business. They had the best food you've ever eaten, but they couldn't stay in business because they didn't know how to market and didn't know how to advertise. Yet I'll guarantee you there are bad restaurants out there that are doing very well, not because they have the best product, but simply because they understand how to market. They understand how to sell. They understand how to advertise.

Let me ask you this one. Do you know how to hire people? Do you know how to fire people? Do you know how to train and manage people? You need to. You can't be in business if you can't do those things.

If you say, "I'll just hire my buddies," or "I'm going to get my family to go in," you are in trouble. Bringing families in is a recipe for disaster, because it's hard to manage family. It's hard to have your mom or your dad or your brother working for you, your kids working for you. What are you thinking? You're stacking the deck against you when you do that.

Your buddies? If you want to destroy your friendship with, hire your buddies, because sooner or later, you're going to have to manage that buddy. That's a hard thing to do.

So ask yourself about your level of experience in hiring, firing, training, and managing.

Then, how are you capitalized? I don't care how much money you put away. There's a rule: it's going to cost you at least twice as much. So you figure out all the money it's going to take for you to start your business, and double it; you still probably won't have enough. I'm betting you're undercapitalized. By the way, if you don't know what *capitalized* means, don't go into business.

How about this? Do you know what a balance sheet is? Confused again? Don't go into business. Do you understand what your real expenses are going to be? Figure out what it's going to cost you, and double that too.

You have to figure out this stuff. There's never enough money. It always takes twice as long, and it always takes twice as much money. It's just a rule. I understand that no matter what project I'm going to start, it's going to take twice as long to accomplish, and it's going to cost me twice as much as I thought it would. If you don't understand that, you are naive, and you have a certain amount of arrogance, because you think you'll be the exception.

Again, if you think you're the exception to the rule, go back and reread the rule. Chances are you're not the exception. If you don't understand that the chances are not in your favor to succeed, but are in your favor to fail, you are naive, and you are arrogant.

People tell you failure is not an option. I hear that all the time; it's what the motivational bozos will say. Listen, failure is always an option, and you'd better be prepared for it. You'd better have a plan B, a plan C, a plan D.

You need to ask yourself this question: What happens when it all goes to hell in a handbasket? What happens when it doesn't work? You'll say, "Oh, but it will." No, chances are it won't. That's the reality of going into business for yourself. Are you prepared for all of these things? Most people aren't. Do you even know the survival rate of the businesses that do what you plan to do? Look it up. I can give you the survival rate of businesses overall, but how about the business you want to start? Do you know the survival rate for that particular industry in the area that you live in? If you don't know that, you're not prepared.

Do you know how to sell? If you don't know how to sell, you can't win. Do you know what sets you apart from your competitor? "I'm better. My food's better." No one cares. If you can't convince me, no one cares. You can't tell me it's better. You have to convince me, and if you blow that experience one time, I'll go to the guy I can count on. The food may not be as good, the experience may not be as good, but I can count on him. Consistency is a big deal. Being good one time doesn't keep you in business. It's being good every time, and that's hard.

Here's the big one. Do you even know if there's a real need, or a market? It's amazing to me that people start into business without analyzing the need and the market. They don't understand even whether there *is* a market. Instead they've listened to their best friend say, "You are so good at this. You ought to do this for a living." Chances are, you shouldn't do it for a living. I mean, really. Chances are you shouldn't.

A lot of work has to happen to make sure you're one of the 5 percent who will succeed. The reason 95 percent fail is that they can't answer the questions I've just asked. Don't be one of the 95 percent. Be one of the 5 percent. Be able to answer these questions correctly. Do the work.

If I could anoint you with a skill that would stack the deck in your favor so your chances of success in business would go way up and you could not only survive but thrive in the marketplace, that skill would be selling. You must be good at selling.

As I've said, no one is going to beat a path to your door. You have to take the product to people. People love to talk about the way selling has changed. I read a lot about that online. I don't believe selling has changed at all.

Selling is, always has been, and always will be about having a product that the customer perceives to be a solution to their problem. It's about solving a problem. If your product doesn't solve a customer's problem, then you have nothing to sell. So ask yourself, what problem does you product or service solve in the minds and lives of the customers you're trying to get?

Then understand this: the bigger the problem you solve, the more you get to charge for it. A 99-cent hamburger solves a 99-cent problem, and a $250,000 heart surgery solves a much bigger problem. That's why it costs so much more.

Have I oversimplified? Not at all. You need to understand that the value the customer places on the problem allows you to set your price of your solution. See how that works? The more the problem costs to the customer, the higher you can set the price of your solution.

You have to be able to pass along that concept. You have to make the customer aware that you have the solution, and then you have to ask him to buy it from you.

I'll give you this: the way people buy has changed. People can now buy over the Internet. People used to have to buy face-to-face. People used to have to come into a brick-and-mortar store and pick the product off the shelf. It doesn't happen that way anymore. I can go online, buy something, and it'll be there by afternoon.

Things have changed in how we buy, but not in how we sell. That's the difference. Selling has always been about the basics, and my basics are this. It's the way I've always sold, and I started my career as a sales trainer, so I'm pretty good at this. Sales comes down to solving a problem. It comes down to making people aware that I have a solution to their problem, and then asking them to buy it. In all the time I'm doing that, I'm working on my product to make sure the value of the problem I solve increases, so I can charge more for it.

That should be your goal too. Solve a problem. Make people aware that you have the solution to the problem, and then ask them to buy it. Try constantly to increase the value of the problem you solve, so you can increase the price of your solution.

Previously I emphasized knowing your core principles for your life. I asked you to figure out what those five core principles for your life were, things that you would never compromise. I'm going to ask you to do the same thing for your business.

Even if you're an employee, I want you to identify what your core principles are. Every business needs to understand the five business principles they will never compromise.

So, get out a sheet of paper and spend a few minutes putting ink to paper to come up with the five core business principles you will never compromise.

Once you've done that, I want you to figure out what it's going to take, a tactical plan, for you to make sure you practice those principles in your business every single day.

4
Money: That Ugly Word

et's get ugly. Let's talk about money. Normally folks don't like to talk about their money unless they have way too much of it. I've also discovered that if there is one area of life where people will lie to you, it's about their money. They don't want to tell you how much they owe, they don't want to tell you how much they have saved, and they certainly don't want to tell you how much they're spending. That is dishonest. I want you to get honest with yourself about your money.

Money takes a bad rap. We've heard all of our life money is the root of all evil. No, money is not the root of all evil. I like money. I enjoy money. I enjoy spending my money. I do think money is to be enjoyed.

That means understanding the proper use of money, and a lot of people don't do that. Money is a measurement of the contribution you make in the marketplace.

Jim Rohn said years ago that people who earn $5 an hour put $5 worth of value into the marketplace, and it takes them an hour to do it. He also said people who earn $5,000 an hour put $5,000 worth of value into the marketplace, and it takes them an hour to do it. The difference is not the hours. The difference is about the amount of value you put in.

Understand first of all that money is a reward for the value you bring. If you're not earning enough money, you're not providing enough value. If you want more money, provide more value. That is something you have to understand to begin with.

The other thing that you have to understand about money is that most people spend too much of it stupidly.

I shot a television show for a few years on A&E called *Big Spender*. It was a reality television show where people would contact us and need help because they were in lots of financial trouble. I would go in and confront them about their spending habits.

Here's what I discovered. For every big spender, there is a big enabler. In fact, I thought the show could have been called *Big Enabler*. People who spend their money typically have somebody who enables them to spend their money, and that typically happens when people don't have a budget.

Here's what I've discovered as well: people who are willing to go on TV and talk about their finances are idiots. You shouldn't want to go on TV and talk about how stupid you've been with your money. That, to me, is just silly. But luckily people were willing to do that, and I was able to teach folks a lot of great lessons as a result of that show.

There were lots of interesting stories on the show. I've dealt with people who had too many fancy cars. One guy had to get rid of a Bentley.

I've also dealt with people who felt so entitled to their cable television that when I told them they had to give it up because they didn't need five HBOs and fourteen Showtimes and seven ESPNs, they got mad. When I explained to a woman that she's not entitled to those, that they are a luxury, she cried and said, "I'm not worth HBO?" No, you're not worth HBO. Your commitment is to your kids and to your bills.

The most interesting experience was shooting the pilot for this show. I had a couple. He didn't have a job. His wife had two jobs. He was just too busy, he said, to go out and look for work. I pointed out to him that he was too lazy to go out and look for work.

As I was standing with this couple in their kitchen, I looked at him. He had a four-year-old son over playing in the corner. I said, "Tell me, do you love your son?"

He said, "Larry, of course I love my son. That's a stupid question to ask me."

"I'm going to call you a liar," I said. Well, now, let me tell you, it'll fire people up when you tell them they're a liar and they don't love their kid. I said, "Let me show you what you really love, but before I do that, let me ask you a couple of questions."

I turned around in his kitchen, I started opening up cabinets, and I said, "If you loved your son, wouldn't your cabinets be full of food? Wouldn't there be cereal here?"

I opened up the refrigerator. I said, "If you loved your son, wouldn't there be juice? Wouldn't there be a half gallon of milk or something in here for your son? If you really loved your son, would there be an eviction notice hanging on your front door? Would you be in the position where they're probably going to come and repossess your car today, so if there was an emergency, you couldn't really do anything about it or would have to take a cab? And you don't have the cash to pay for that. If you really loved your son, would your household be in this kind of situation?

"Instead let me show you what you love," I said. I pulled open a drawer in his kitchen and pulled out five cartons of cigarettes. "This is what you love. You love this more than your son." Then I scraped the five cartons of cigarettes onto the floor and stomped them all with my cowboy boot.

He came across the counter and acted like a big old tough guy, and I said, "Back off, and realize what I'm telling you. You love your cigarettes more than you love the idea of making sure that your son is properly cared for. That is the reality of the situation."

As I've already told you, your money goes to what's important to you. It was more important for him to have cigarettes than it was for his son to have milk in the refrigerator, more important than paying his rent, more important than making his car payment. It was more important for his wife to work two jobs than it was for him to work one job.

I've worked a lot with people over the years to help them determine what their priorities are. You need to determine what your priorities are for your money as well. It's very simple. If you still use a checkbook, get out your checkbook. Or go online and look at your bank statement. Pull out your credit-card statement. Look at where your money goes.

What are you spending your money on? That will tell you what's important to you. Stop lying to yourself. This will be the truth. This will be the cold, hard truth looking at you from a sheet of paper or a computer screen and telling you what's really important in your life.

By the way, never believe that money isn't important. Money is important. If you don't think it is, grow up not having any money, or find yourself in a situation where you don't have any money.

I grew up poor. Won't say I was dirt-poor, but I was dusty. We didn't have very much at all. It was a good thing we had a big garden, and we had chickens, and we raised our own meat. That's how we ate, and that's how we lived.

My parents never made much money, and we never had a whole lot of stuff. I never really realized quite how poor we were until I was in the eighth grade. I walked into my civics class, and a kid looked up at me and said, "Winget, are you so poor, you only have one pair of blue jeans?"

It was true. I only had one pair of blue jeans, and they had a rip in the pocket, and all of your blue jeans can't have the same rip in the same pocket. So I was busted, and I was embarrassed. I was thirteen years old, and I had just been embarrassed publicly in front of a bunch of thirteen-year-old girls, and that made it even harder. No teenager wants to be humiliated in front of his classmates, especially in front of a bunch of little girls.

My mind clicked at that very moment. I decided that my life was going to be different. I was never going to be made fun of for being broke again. That was a commitment I made to myself at that moment. I decided I would figure out a way to get rich.

Now here was the problem. I didn't have any rich role models. There weren't a whole lot of rich people in Muskogee, Oklahoma. I certainly didn't have my parents as role models. My parents were responsible with their money. They just didn't have much of it.

I didn't know what rich really looked like except from watching television, because there wasn't a lot going on in Muskogee. I decided the one skill I had that I could utilize, even though I didn't have any money, was that I could work harder than anybody else.

I could always outwork you. I may not be smarter than you, but I can outwork you. I can show up earlier, I can stay later, I can work between my breaks. I can outwork anybody. I don't care who you are; I can outwork you. That was the commitment I made to myself, because I was taught to regard hard work and excellence as the key to being successful.

So whenever I got a job, I outworked everybody. Consequently I got raises faster than other people. I got more opportunities than other people. When I got a job selling, I thought that was the goose that laid the golden egg. I could make as much money as I wanted based on how hard I was willing to work, how many people I was willing to call on, how much

I was willing to sell, because I got a commission. If you tell me there's a commission available and that my income is going to be based on calling on people, I can call on lots of them. I outworked everybody, and I did pretty well. I really did.

People ask me today why I dress funny. If you've never seen a picture of me, go online and look up "Larry Winget." I wear wild cowboy shirts and wild cowboy boots. Let me tell you why. I do that because I grew up poor watching TV. On Saturday afternoons I used to watch Porter Wagoner with my grandmother.

If you've never seen Porter Wagoner, he was the original king of bling. He wore rhinestone suits that were sparkling, and had big wagon wheels. It was Porter Wagoner and the Wagonmasters. He had suits with big wagon wheels and cactus on them and bright embroidery and rhinestones.

I used to sit there in front of that little TV when I was a kid, and I said, "I bet that's how rich people dress. If I ever get rich, I'm going to dress like that." Many years later, I realized I was rich, and I was going to start dressing like that. So I threw away the suits and bought cowboy shirts. I already had a bunch of cowboy boots, but I kind of went wild. Now I have over 100 custom pairs of cowboy boots and 400 cowboy shirts. I dress the way I want to. I earned the right to do that.

That was a measurement of my success. What's your measurement of success? You have one. This is something I learned while I was doing *Big Spender.* I had a woman who had seventy-five or eighty pairs of shoes. That's fine. That's not that out of line. The problem was she didn't have any money and was going in debt to buy them. She turned on me one day and said, "Are you kidding me? I've been online and looked at your closet. You have 100 pairs of custom cowboy boots. How is it OK for you to have 100 pairs of custom cowboy boots, and you're giving me a bad time about seventy-five pairs of shoes?"

"There's a big difference," I said. "I can afford it."

You can have whatever you want as long as you can afford it. It's when all your bills are paid. It's when you have investments. It's when you have savings. After you've saved, and after you've invested, and after you've paid all of your commitments, if you have money left over, and you would like to treat yourself, I have no problem with that. My problem is when people put treating themselves in front of their commitments.

Few people do save. Sadly, two-thirds of people in my generation—the fifty-five to sixty-four-year-olds—don't have any money saved for retirement.

The average fifty-year-old in America has $2,500. Do the math. You have $2,500 at fifty years old. Let's say you've been working for at least twenty-five years. (Most people go to work before they're twenty-five, or at least they used to). You have $2,500 saved. That's $100 a year, $8.33 a month, $2 a week. That's the best you've been able to do.

You're an idiot. That's just what it comes down to. You had bad priorities. You've made mistakes. You were stupid when it came to your money. However, I bet if I went to your house, if I looked at your life-style, I could figure out where all that money went.

Your priority was not saving. Your priority was not being financially stable. Your priority was self-indulgence.

Let me tell you the fastest way to get past self-indulgence: operate with a budget.

Part of living the politically incorrect lifestyle is the ability to be incredibly free, to have true inde-pendence, to be the way you want to be, not to rely on somebody else at all times.

If you want freedom, if you want independence, it's about getting control of your money. Part of get-ting control of your money, even when you don't have any, is to operate with a plan. We've already talked about the importance of a plan in your per-sonal life and in your business, but you need a plan for your money, and that is what a budget is.

I've become known as a personal-finance guy. Having worked with people on their finances for the last fifteen years or so, I have yet to find one who has a written budget. Not one. If I ask people how much they owe, they don't have a clue. If I ask people how much they earn, many of them don't have a clue. If I ask them what their monthly expenses are, they don't have a clue.

How can you expect to run a business without a plan? How can you expect to run a successful life without a plan, and how do you expect to be financially secure when you have no written plan for your money?

It's very important for you to get a budget so you know how much you have to work with, how much you owe, whom you owe it to, and when it's due. It's also important to understand the proper way to use your money when you get it.

Let me give you a very simple guideline. When you get paid, save 10 percent off the top. Then invest 10 percent. Then be charitable with 10 percent. In religious circles, they call that a tithe. Call it what you want to. If you're not religious, don't call it a tithe. I just call it the right thing to do. There are people in this world who do need help, and it's the right thing to do to be charitable with your money. So save 10 percent, invest 10 percent, be charitable with 10 percent, and learn to live on 70 percent.

If you're reading this book early in your life, these are good numbers to work with. If you're reading this midway through your life, you may want to adjust those numbers, because if you're at a high-earning point in your life (midway through, let's say), you need to be investing more and saving more. If you're coming at this later in life, you probably need to be living on much less, investing much more, and saving much more.

The problem is, as people age, they're not prepared. When they think about what might happen when they retire, they think in terms of the government.

Folks, let's get realistic. The government's broke. Turn on any news channel at any time of the day and you probably will find that rolling debt clock on one of them. We are trillions and trillions of dollars in debt. Right now we are deeply in debt to China. We are spending more money as a country than we take in. Interesting—most people are in pretty much the same situation. They are deeply in debt. They owe somebody else everything they have, and they are spending more money than they take in.

Since that is the situation in our country, you cannot count on the fact that the government, meaning Social Security and Medicare and Medicaid, are going to be there for you when you retire. My suggestion for everyone is this: *earn enough money that you never have to rely on anyone.*

At this point we have too many seniors who simply don't have the ability to retire. A recent study said that half of our seniors know they're going to have to work at least part-time in order to be able to survive. Most people who are in their mid-forties right now understand that Social Security will probably be bankrupt by the time they get around to drawing it. So they're not going to be able to count on it.

You can only count on yourself, which means you have to get to work. Here's what I suggest you do: educate yourself about money. It's amazing how few people know anything about money and the way money works in our market, government, debt, and so forth.

I used to do a regular show on Saturday mornings on the Fox Business Channel on which we took callers with questions about their finances. One morning I was there with a bunch of Wall Street and investor types; I'm the regular guy in the cowboy shirt. A guy called in and said that the Dow had dropped 180 points. "Larry, what do you think?"

All those guys jumped in, and they started going through all the things that he should do in terms of the Dow dropping and what that meant in the marketplace and what that meant to our country and blah, blah, blah.

I listened, and finally it was my turn, even though he had called in asking for me. I said, "Let me ask you a question. Do you know what the Dow is?"

"No, I don't," he said.

"Do you have any money in the stock market?"

"No, I don't."

"Then why are you asking this question?" He really didn't know why. He just wanted to know what it meant when the Dow dropped 180 points.

Then I asked him, "Do you have any credit-card debt?"

"Yes, I do," he said.

"Let me give you the highest return on your money you will ever find," I said. "Pay off your credit cards. That is a guaranteed rate of return. You're not going to find a guaranteed rate of return any place else. Pay off your credit cards."

Here's a guy who has fallen victim to the news cycle. He is paying more attention to the news than to his own finances. He's panicking and trying to figure out what's going on in the marketplace when he doesn't have any money in the market. Most importantly, he's sitting there with a lot of credit-card debt.

How about you? Do you know what the stock market is really all about? Do you know what the Dow is? Do you know what it means when the news says the country's in a debt crisis? Are you educated at all financially?

Let me suggest that you go out and read about all that, because more than ever we need a society that is educated in finances. We need voters who understand the importance of voting about the debt and about the problem our country is in right now because we have so much debt.

We need an educated citizenry. We need a society that understands debt, understands investments, understands saving. The least you can do for yourself and for your family moving forward is to get educated.

In terms of your own personal finances, here's the first thing I want you to do: complete a budget. Pull out a sheet of paper and write down how much money you have coming in, and when it comes in. Is it weekly? Is it monthly? Figure out what your expenses are.

Look at your debt. Figure out all the payments that are due versus how much money you have coming in. Then subtract your expenses from your income, and hopefully that turns out to be a positive number. If you don't know what a positive number is, we already have a problem, because the opposite of a positive number would be a negative number, which means you are spending more than you are bringing in. You're spending more than you are earning. That means you're upside down, folks, and you have a problem.

If it makes you feel any better, and it shouldn't, 43 percent of Americans spend more money than they earn.

Pay close attention to what I've just said: spend more money than they *earn*. A lot of people would say, spend more money than they *make*.

Get this straight about money. You don't make money. You're not the Mint. You don't print money. You earn money. Your money is an exchange for the value you bring to the marketplace.

Do you see how all these things build on top of one another? It's always going to come down to that. So I want you to figure out who you owe and how much you have. Hopefully, you are spending less than you earn. If you're not, here's what I want you to do.

Do your best to get out of all of your silly debt, and silly debt is credit-card debt. That means you have to, one, change your spending habits. The best thing you can do is start to track your money on a daily basis. Track every penny. If you have to write it down in a little journal, write it down. If you think you can keep it on your smartphone, do it that way, but track your money.

You need to know where all of the stupid money goes. We all spend stupid money. Stupid money is when you pull into the gas station, fill your tank up, and say, "I could really use one of those giant Slurpees inside. I could use a candy bar." You go in and you buy them.

You don't need to do that. Trust me, most people are fat: they don't need that candy bar, and they don't need a giant soda. That was a silly expense. It's dumb to do that. And let me tell you what you don't understand: when you buy that, you'll put it on your credit card along with your gasoline. You won't realize it was stupid money, and at the end of the month you'll say that was a gas expense. No, it wasn't a gas expense. It was a stupid expense.

Start to tally it up, and at the end of the month see how much money you've spent in that stupid column. I want you to know how much you spent on gas and groceries, on your utilities, on your car and insurance, and all of that. Of course, that's what a budget really is, but I want you to focus first on the stupid money you spent on things you didn't need, but you just wanted.

There is a huge difference between needs and wants. If you're in trouble, most financial people would tell you to focus only on needs. I'm going way past that. You can convince yourself that you need things you really don't need. They're just wants.

I have three categories, not two. I have needs, wants, and can't-live-withouts. If you can't live without it, that's where your money goes first. What is a can't-live-without? Shelter and food. So let's look at those.

Are you living above your means in terms of your shelter? If you're really in trouble financially, you might want to look at that. Here's an easier one that will be a harder habit for you to break. How are you doing in terms of spending money on your food? Typically, the average American these days spends about $2,500 a year on eating out.

You could fix that number. Say you just cut that in half. (See, I'm not that tough a guy after all.) Just cut it in half. You've saved $1,200 by yourself. As a couple, you've saved $2,400. As a family of four, you've saved a lot of money. For a family of five, it's over $10,000 a year.

What could you do with that $10,000 in preparing yourself for the future, retirement, for your kids' college education? There's a lot of things you could do, but you're going to have to discipline yourself, and you're going to have to alter your lifestyle. You're going to have to give some things up. You're going to have to think differently and spend differently.

Food and shelter—those are the things you can't live without. Past that, it comes to commitments. Commitments are your bills. Those are the contracts that you signed, meaning credit-card debt, utilities, mortgage, car payment, the deals you made.

As I've said, I have some basic beliefs. My belief is a deal is a deal. When you said you would do it, you do it. I don't care how difficult it is for you to do it, you do it. You gave your word you would do it. Would you want somebody to break a written contract with you? Then why are you late on your car payment? Why are you not making all of your credit-card payments?

Those are contracts—written, legal contracts. You signed your name on a document that said you would pay at least this amount of money on this date, and you aren't doing it. You know what that makes you? It makes you a liar. Oh, that's politically incorrect, isn't it?

Some people would say, "Larry, that just means I had different priorities this month." No, you're just a liar. You said you would make that payment, and you didn't do it. Look yourself in the eye in the mirror and say, "I'm a liar. I don't keep my word."

You wouldn't want somebody to do that with you if they owed you money. You'd raise hell and get on the phone, or you'd go knock on their door, or you'd confront them in some way. Yet if you're behind on your bills and somebody calls you, you're upset. You say, "How dare they call me!" Because it's their money. They loaned you that money, and you agreed to pay them, and now you're not, and you don't think they have the right to collect.

Today we've made it hard for people to collect their money. We should make it easier. Let me ask you this. Did anybody hold a gun to your head and say, "Buy this?" No. You bought that by choice. You chose to spend your money on that new shirt, that new suit, that new dress, those new shoes. Nobody made you do it. It was your choice, and now that choice is a commitment. It's a deal you made, and the people who fronted you that money expected you to keep your end of the bargain. When you don't, don't get mad at them, get mad at yourself. Realize that you're responsible.

You'll be much less likely to spend in an out-of-control fashion if you operate from a budget, because you'll know how much discretionary money you have. Again I'm going to go back to that statistic: 43 percent of people spend more money than they earn. There is no discretionary money. If you're in that category, what does that mean you do? You pay down your expenses until you have discretionary money again.

My goal, number one, is for you to pay off your credit-card debt. They have the highest interest, and they are the things that will hurt you the most in the long run, because those are the first people to report on your credit history.

Believe me, your credit history is important. I recently got a letter from a woman who asked me a question about credit history. She said, "I never plan on owning a home."

By the way, that's a growing trend among millennials. They have no interest in owning a home. They saw it become a problem for their parents, who overbought and couldn't afford what they had, so they lost their houses in the recession, and now most millennials say they're not interested in owning a home.

This woman said, "I don't have any interest in owning a home, and I don't need any credit. I live very minimally, and so what difference does it make if I protect my credit history?" She went on to say that she had a very poor credit history because she had been stupid in the past, but she had no interest in fixing it. She said, "Why don't you do us all a favor, Larry, and tell us our credit history doesn't matter if we don't ever plan on owning anything?"

Naivete screamed from this letter. You have no idea how important your credit history is for getting a job. Your credit history will in part determine whether an employer hires you or not.

Do you realize that your credit history will determine how much you pay for auto insurance, for life insurance? Look it up if you don't believe I'm right. You will discover that insurance companies can determine how likely you are to file claims based on your credit history, because people who have a lower credit score typically file more claims. This makes them a higher risk, which means their rates will be higher.

A lot will be determined on the basis of your credit score. You need to protect it. There are two things we will never be without—our reputation and our credit score—and you can destroy both of those things in a minute. Protect your reputation just as you protect your credit score, and protect your credit score as if it's your reputation, because it is.

I also suggest that you carry cash. I've always been a big believer in cash. I believe cash is a way to make sure that you'll spend less. One problem in society is we've made it too easy to spend money, and we never realize when it's gone. If you use a debit card for everything, if you use a credit card for everything, the money is harder to keep track of. You don't know where or how you've spent it.

I know there are lots of apps that can track your spending for you; people love to tell me they can rely on them. I am not buying it, folks. The financial condition of most citizens right now in America doesn't prove that to be the fact.

Another problem is that you can pay with your phone. I know people love doing that, and I know it's cool, but get past the cool factor and get back to your level of willpower and your level of discipline. Do you have the discipline to make sure that you still have plenty of money and that you aren't spending outside your budget?

Do you have the willpower to say no to things if all it takes is waving your phone across the top of a pad? I'm not even sure I do.

Let me give you an example of what I'm talking about. I was recently in the airport, and I was behind a lady in line at a little shop there. I was buying a bottle of water to carry with me. She was buying a big candy bar. First of all, a candy bar costs a lot of money in an airport—a couple of bucks. She's standing in line, and she hands the clerk her credit card. Second, if you're buying a candy bar on a credit card because you don't have two $1 bills in your pocket, that alone ought to tell you that you don't need the candy bar. I could also tell by looking at this woman that she did not need this candy bar, but she was buying it, and she gave the clerk her credit card. It was declined.

The clerk was very nice and said, "Ma'am, I'm sorry. This one won't go through."

She shook her head and said, "Try it again." It's always funny to me how people get defensive when they're broke. They want to blame the credit card, or the poor clerk, who is just as embarrassed for you as you ought to be for yourself. The woman got mad at the clerk and at the credit-card company. But I'll guarantee you that she didn't have any money in her account.

She turned to me and said, "What am I supposed to do?"

I was standing behind her, looking like Larry Winget, and I said, "Maybe you ought to just do without that candy bar."

She just stared a hole through me and said, "Oh, you're that guy, aren't you?" She recognized me.

"Yup, I'm that guy," I said. "You don't need that candy bar, and you don't need to be buying it on a credit card." She got mad, threw the candy bar down, and stomped out.

You may be saying, "Larry, you had no right to tell her she didn't need it." Folks, she didn't need it. Her credit card wouldn't clear $2, and if you're buying a candy when you don't need it financially, I'm betting you don't need it physically as well.

The problem is she saw that candy as a need. It wasn't a need. It was a want, and she certainly could have lived without it.

When you're pulling out your credit card, make sure that you have a plan. (Oh, it's funny how we keep going back to a plan.) Make sure you have a plan to get that credit card paid off.

I am not like many of the financial guys out there, who will tell you that all credit is bad and that credit cards are evil. I do not believe credit cards are evil. I believe credit-card abuse is evil, and to me, the abuse of a credit card is charging something you don't need that you can live without and you don't have the ability to pay off when the bill comes in.

Carrying cash is an easier way for you to know when you don't have any money. If you've spent the cash that you have allotted for the week on things that you are allowed to spend cash out of your pocket, let's say lunch or a candy bar, when it's gone, it's gone.

I am very pro-cash. With something that's only electronic, you don't always understand when it's gone. Recently a person said, "Larry, you are just setting yourself up to be mugged." Listen, if I get mugged, I'd rather hand the mugger a handful of cash. I want something to give that guy. I want him to feel he's getting something for mugging me so he won't hurt me. I'd rather give him some cash than a debit card and say, "I hope there's something left on it."

People will come up with all these weak excuses. They're looking for a reason to argue with me. It always comes down to whether you can afford it or not. You ought to be able to have the money to buy what you afford. Money, to me, is green, it folds, and it goes in your pocket or your wallet.

One of the biggest excuses people give me is, "I grew up poor, Larry. I don't know anything about money. This is the way it's always been for me."

I understand growing up poor. I've been there. I grew up poor, but that's not an excuse to stay poor. If you're born poor, that's not your fault. If you die poor, that *is* your fault. You can go out there, go to work, live beneath your means, and save some money so you don't have to die poor. This is still the land of many opportunities, but you have to be willing to do what it takes to take advantage of those opportunities.

Stop using that "I grew up poor." It's victim mentality—the world has done this to you, it's through no fault of your own that you still don't have any money. I understand there are poor people, but *poor* is a condition, and *broke* is a situation. You need to fix your situation before it becomes your condition. If you're broke right now, fix your spending. Work on your income. Change your lifestyle so you don't have to die poor.

If you don't have the education to do that, read a book. There are plenty of books out there on how to get yourself financially secure and out of debt. I wrote one called *You're Broke Because You Want to Be*. How's that for politically incorrect?

People say, "I don't want to be financially strapped." Yes, you do. If you didn't want to be that way, you'd be another way. Simple as that. Every situation in your life must be the way you want it to be; otherwise it would be different. If you don't want to be broke, stop being broke, and stop using that victim mentality as an excuse.

Also stop convincing yourself that you need everything that you see. Everything that's shiny, you think you want. There's so much stupid reality TV out there now that people think they actually can keep up with the Kardashians. You can't keep up with them. Stop thinking you deserve to keep up with them or with anybody else you see on television.

Stop trying to keep up with the people next door. The problem with that old keep-up-with-the-Joneses thing is that the Joneses are broke. Everything they have is mortgaged, they're deeply in debt, and they have no money. So you're trying to keep up with people you should not be admiring in any way.

Stop living for the approval of other people. I've already talked about this in your personal life, but it certainly applies to your money. You shouldn't care what anybody thinks. You should care more about being financially secure.

When your bills are paid, you don't owe anybody any money, you have cash in your pocket and money in the bank, your retirement is secure, and you have investments that will carry you to the day you die, that's something to be proud of. If you want to gloat about what a big dog you are, you can gloat about that.

Some people give me this excuse: "Larry, you just don't understand. I'm too busy to earn more money." Really? You're so busy you can't do a little more? Here's what I've discovered. If you do a little more, you get a little more. If you're a farmer and you plant a little more seed, you reap a few more crops. That's the way it works.

Here's what works sometimes. Sometimes you can do a little more, and you get a whole lot more. How does that work? Beats me. It just works. So do a little more. Everybody has the ability to do that. What could you do that would allow you to earn a little bit more money?

People have said to me, "Larry, haven't you heard, don't you watch TV?" Yes, folks, I watch TV. I'm *on* TV. "Do you not understand that things cost more than they used to, and yet wages are stagnant?" I've heard all of those things. It is politically correct for you to bring those things up, but I'm telling you that's all a load of bung.

I'm not saying that it's not true. I'm saying if you're using that as an excuse for not doing well, you're lying to yourself. You're looking for an excuse, and people who want an excuse will grasp for anything. You're grasping at all of those buzzwords of the day so you'll have an excuse for not doing well.

If you're not doing well, it's your fault. There are plenty of opportunities out there. Don't buy into the idea that folks just can't do well anymore. We're increasing wealth faster than we ever have in history—for the people who are willing to get out there and bust their butt and make it happen.

If you are willing to stay stuck in the middle, then you'll stay stuck in the middle. If you're willing to be at the bottom, believe me, there's plenty of room at the bottom. Lots of people are down there with you at the bottom, but for those people who are unwilling to accept their current financial lives and are willing to do whatever it takes to fix them, there are still fortunes to be made.

Here's a word of warning. When you have decided that you want more money in your life, there are going to be lots of people there who will tell you that it's easy to do and offer you a get-rich-quick scheme. There's more of that than ever before going on, mainly because it can be promoted so easily by way of the Internet.

Many people will say, "If you'll just buy my program, I will teach you how to make this much money." I'm telling you: be wary. People who tell you that you can get rich by buying their program are normally the ones who make all the money from the program, not the people who are taking it.

Do your research. Don't fall victim to people who are there with their hands out saying, "Pay me money, and I'll teach you how to be rich." Rich happens, but rich happens in a very slow way. It comes from doing the right thing, serving people well, being the right kind of business that customers want to share their money and their time with.

Be the right kind of manager, who attracts the right kind of employee, so you can build your business with them. Very few fortunes are made overnight these days, yet there are people who will make grandiose promises to you. I have learned to be very wary of those people. Make sure that they can really back it up. As I've already said, if you're going into business, and you're looking at buying into a company, ask the tough questions. Ask them how many people have really done this, and how many people have *not* been able to do this. There are too many people out there who are full of great words.

The Internet is famous for hype these days. I can say whatever I want to say about myself on the Internet, and there will be some idiot who will believe it. We have become much too gullible about what we read on the Internet and what we hear on the infomercials.

It's smart to be careful with your hard-earned money. Riches normally take some time to earn. You don't become a millionaire overnight, regardless of what these bozos tell you.

One of the biggest mistakes you can ever make—and it's hard to go back—is falling victim to one of these schemes, because they don't offer any money-back guarantees. Once you've spent it, it's over. They have it, and you don't. You're stuck with lousy results, and you're upset. It was your own gullibility that got you in this mess. Be wary.

* * *

Now, again, take a sheet of paper and write down some money-mastery principles that you're not willing to compromise. Write down some ideas that, from this point on in your life, you are going to keep as core values when it comes to your money.

Here's one suggestion. Never compromise saving. Always save some money right off the top. Don't compromise that. You could use that to start your list of five.

Here's another excuse I often hear: "Larry, you don't understand. Do you not realize that some people in the world just have more than others? Haven't you heard of the haves and the have-nots? I'm just one of the have-nots." Boy, have you said that to the wrong guy.

We all grow up believing that the world is full of the haves and the have-nots. That's not true. The world is full of the wills and the will-nots. Will you do what it takes in order to get what you want? Will you do what it takes in order to be one of the haves?

I recently posted this on social media. Somebody came after me hard on this one and said I was full of it for saying that life is full of the haves and the have-nots. Do I not understand about Third World countries? I'm not talking about Third World countries. I'm talking about you right now.

Let's get clear about the haves and the have-nots. Reverend Ike was a money preacher back in the eighties and nineties. He said, "Make fun of the rich, and you'll never be one of us." I like that line.

If your goal is to have more money, why would you put down people who do? Why would you put down the people who have worked hard to earn their way? That's dumb. All you're doing is setting yourself up for criticism once you do earn the money.

Here's the other deal. The haves are the people who provide the jobs for the wills, and the haves are the ones who end up paying the taxes that support the will-nots.

5 Integrity, Friends, and Family

You cannot be successful is life only by being successful in business or with money. You know why? There are people involved. You also have to learn how to be successful in your relationships.

Just like in other areas of your life, being successful in relationships starts with you. You will attract the kind of people into your life on the basis of who you are as a person. If you're a mean person, you're probably going to attract mean people into your life, because why would nice, wonderful, loving people want to hang around a jerk?

You surround yourself with people in your life who are most like you. You attract people who are like you. If you want to attract good people in your life, become a better person. If you want to attract rich people in your life, start figuring out what would be attractive to rich people. If you want to attract smarter people in your life, what would smarter people be doing? Where would they be going? I bet they would probably be in bookstores so they could be improving themselves.

It's really very simple. Figure out the kind of people you want to have in your life, and do your best to become that kind of person. That way you will attract that kind of person into your life. Amazing how all of this starts with fixing yourself first.

Ask yourself what you need to do to change who you are so you would be attractive to the kind of people you want in your life. When you do that, you will be amazed at the improvement in the quality of your relationships.

Let's get specific. Look at your friends. As I mentioned earlier, how much money you will make depends on the quality of friends you have in your life. Your income is going to be on average of the incomes of your five closest friends. If you want to make more money, perhaps you should surround yourself with people who make more money.

The same thing applies in other areas. Look at your friends and decide where they are moving you. Yes, your friends move you along. Are they people who will coddle you, put their arms around you, and say, "Honey, it's a cold, cruel world out there. No wonder you're having such a hard time." I don't believe that's a real friend. I don't think that person is moving your closer to where you want to be. I think they're keeping you stuck and dragging you backward.

To me, a true friend will put their arm around you and say, "You're being an idiot. You deserve better than this. You are worth more than this. I know you can do better than this. I believe in you." Then they will encourage you to be your best self. A good friend is hard on you. They're tough. A good friend loves you enough to be that way.

People who want to blame others for your circumstances are not your friends. Shy away from those people. Look at the quality of friends you have right now. Run through all your best buddies. Run through their names in your mind. What are they doing for you? Are they coddling you, or are they being tough on you and making you be better as a person? Hopefully it's the latter.

Where do your friends have you going? Maybe that's a tough one for you to answer. Think about it, though. Do they only have you going out and spending your money? Are they enablers? Do they just have you going to the bar and having fun? I have nothing against going to the bar and having fun, but is that all they have you doing?

Do they have you going to the gym so you can exercise and be healthier? What do they have you reading? (Is the first thing you say, "Reading?" That's a clue.) Where do they have you going?

Then ask yourself this: What do you talk about with your friends? Do you just talk about other people? Do you only gripe and complain and whine when you're around one another? Do you sit around and moan and groan about how bad it is out there in the world? Or do you talk about things you could do that would make your life more fun, better, more enjoyable, so you could have more and do more and be more?

In other words, are your friends moving you closer to where you want to be, or are they moving you farther away from where you want to be?

The only way to determine that is to already be clear about where you want to be. When you know where you want to be, when your priorities are clear, when you know what's important to you in life, when you have identified your core values, it's pretty easy to look at the people and relationships in your life and ask, "Are these people helping me achieve what's important to me?" If they're not, walk away. Move them out of your life.

How do you do that? For me, it's pretty simple. It comes down to saying this: "You're not moving me closer to where I want to be in my life. You're hurting me more than you're helping me. I need to limit our access to each other. We won't be talking anymore."

See how easy that was? You think, "That's rude." No, what's rude is allowing people to keep you from achieving your goal. That's being rude to yourself. In fact, that's stupid.

Why would you ever let anyone stand between you and what is best for you, your family, your money, your health? Why would you allow that? You have to learn to be tough on those people you surround yourself with. Just as you expect them to be tough on you. That's the basis of true friendship.

Now ask yourself what kind of a friend you are. Are you the kind of friend that will commiserate? Are you the kind of friend who will sit around and gripe and moan and complain with your buddies, or are you the kind of friend who's a real friend and say, "I think you can do better than this. I believe in you, I'm going to encourage you. You're being an idiot right now, and I know you can do better"? Are you that kind of a friend? I hope so.

So being a good friend and having good friends is really very simple. It comes down to identifying your core values. If you surround yourself with people who can lead you in any direction, it's because you have not drawn the line in the concrete that says, "This is what I will put up with, and this is what I won't put up with." When you do that, it will help you find and attract the right kind of people into your life.

By the way, these days the word *friend* means something totally different from what it used to. You know what I'm going to blame for that? Facebook. You can have 5,000 friends. I have 5,000 of them; I have since Facebook started.

I bet I don't know 4,950 of them. I really don't even know who they are. I might know the other fifty, and probably only five to ten of those are actually friends. But these days we judge ourselves based on social media, that is, on the quantity of our friends, instead of the quality of our friendship.

Stop considering people who interact with you on social media as your friends. They're not your friends just because they follow you on Twitter or on Facebook, or they've made a connection with you on LinkedIn. If they follow you on Instagram and put a little heart on a picture that you've posted, that does not mean that they're your friends.

Stop trying to make those friends happy. Go back to what's really important to you in your life: making yourself happy. When you focus on that, you'll surround yourself with true friends, not those make-believe ones on social media.

Let's talk about the politically incorrect approach to marriage, to having a partner, a spouse. I believe it's a little different than what we've been told, and I believe the definition is changing all the time. We watch television shows and movies, and they give us the idea that it takes another person to make us feel whole. We've seen movies use lines like, "You complete me."

Let me be very clear about this: You don't complete me. Two halves do not make a whole. It takes two whole, complete people to come together into a relationship and actually make it work. Nothing is accomplished by two partial human beings together trying to make one. Half plus half equals one. One plus one equals two. Two is stronger. That's the way you have to start to think.

So don't come into a relationship as a partial person. Your goal is to come into a relationship as a whole, complete person. Don't look to another human being to fulfill you. The only thing another human being can do is complement you. They add to you. Maybe they are much different from you, which is fine, but they still complement who you are.

It's said that opposites attract. That's true: opposites do attract. Not for long, because at some point those opposites have to find things in common that keep them interested, that keep the conversation going.

I've been married over thirty years. I think about my wife and me. We could not be more different. It's a challenge for us every single day, just as it is for most married couples who are willing to be honest.

You have to work to be married. You can't be lazy. I see too many people who get lazy when they get married or find a partner. You see them too. Walk through the mall.

You see a couple. Say they've gone out for dinner. She's done her best to look very nice that evening. She's put on her little black dress and her high heels; she's done her hair and put her makeup on, and he's put on his cleanest dirty T-shirt. He's wearing his flip-flops and shorts. I guess he didn't get the notice that long pants were more appropriate for this particular restaurant. He looks as if he doesn't care. He's not trying to make anybody happy. He's making himself happy. He certainly isn't trying to make his wife happy.

You look at the couple and say, "Did they not have a discussion before they decided where to go to dinner?" The guy's wife should have turned to him and said, "Oh, no. You're not dressing like that. Have you not looked at me? I put forth the effort, out of respect for myself and for you and for where we're going to look nice. I expect the same from you. Get in there, clean up, shave, and change."

We get lazy in relationships, and we start taking each other for granted. That's one thing that kills a relationship faster than any other.

The other day somebody asked me what I liked best about my wife. That's very simple: what I like best about my wife is that she likes me. I'm not an easy man to like. I'm not an easy man to live with. The fact that she has chosen to live with me and put up with me—I find that amazing, and I'm very appreciative. I never take that for granted at all, because if I'm not there to remind myself how hard I am to get along with, everybody else is. So when I find a person who's willing to put up with me and love me in spite of myself, I appreciate that.

I look at my wife and me, and I look at other couples, and I realize that most of them focus on being in love. After all these years, I will readily admit that my wife and I had a tough patch. Most couples do at some point in their lives. They have a time when it just gets hard, and you have to question whether you're willing to put up with it or whether you just want to say no, call it quits, and start over in another direction.

What kept us together, and what helped us to last for many years, is we realized that loving each other is not as important as liking each other. I could have walked away from my marriage. I could have divorced my wife. I could never have walked away from my best friend. My wife is my best friend. We have a great relationship because we're solid friends.

We do everything for each other as friends that I spoke about above. We're tough on each other. We expect the best from each other. We encourage each other as friends. We read books and talk about the books we read. We enjoy doing the same things. I help her achieve her goals; she helps me achieve mine. She moves me closer to where I want to be in life, and hopefully I do the same for her. She is my friend. I could never give up my friend. I could walk away from my marriage, but my marriage is based in friendship.

The problem is people fall in love, and they never build a friendship. I see people who walk away from their partners or from their husbands or from their wives, and they say, "I don't love them anymore." Who cares?

A relationship is much more than the passion of being in love. Being in love takes a lot of work, and besides, I've discovered most people just aren't that loveable. Certainly they're not that lovable in the long term. So look at your relationship with your spouse, and say, "Do I like her or him?" That's the most important thing, because that's what's going to carry you in the long term.

Let me give you a couple of hints about that. When you ask yourself, "Do I like this person?" and you're having trouble answering that question, go back to a list. (I'm big on making lists.) Pull out a sheet of paper, and write down what you do like about them.

Here's what I've discovered. If you focus on what you like about that person, you will see more of it in that person. If you reward what you like in that person, you will certainly see more of it.

My wife and I are helpful to each other. One of my favorite things is to be shaving in the morning and having her walk in, set a cup of coffee down next to me, and walk on. I really like that. Every once in a while I stop and say, "This is one of my favorite things; this is the sweetest thing you do for me, and I appreciate that." You know what happens? The coffee shows up every single day.

Does that mean my wife is my waitress? That's not what I'm saying at all. I'm saying that when she does something out of love for me, and I compliment her for it, I acknowledge that she's done it. I know that she did it purely out of love for me, and when I reward her for that, what's magical is that it shows up more often in my life.

She tells me, "Larry, you know what I really like? I never have to ask you to carry out the trash. You are on top of it. You just do that. I hear wives complaining about their husbands. They never do anything around the house. They won't carry out the trash. They won't clean up the table after dinner. I never have to ask you. It's just done."

Is it my job to carry out the trash more than it's her job? I don't know, but it's something I don't mind doing, and I'd just as soon do it as have her do it. I feel comfortable doing it, and because she appreciates and acknowledges it in our relationship, I will hustle to make sure that the trash is carried out.

Those are little things, but those little things are what matter in relationships, especially when you're in it for the long haul. You don't remember the big things, I promise you, you don't. We never forget the little niceties that we bestow on each other.

I encourage you to make a list of what you like about the person you live with, your spouse, your partner. Keep those things fresh in your mind all the time, and don't be so worried or focused that you don't love them every minute of the day.

Love is like passion. It's fleeting. Friendship, which you work on to maintain, is rooted in holding each other up and encouraging them to be the best version of who they are. That's what lasts.

Let me tell you a story. I was sitting on an airplane, flying back one evening from Las Vegas. I was in the aisle seat. I was in the middle of working on my first book, *Shut Up, Stop Whining, and Get a Life*, and I was typing away on my laptop. An old couple was sitting in the middle seat and the window seat next to me. I mean a really old couple.

As I was typing, the gentleman, who was in the middle seat, leaned over and looked at my laptop. I had just typed the line, "A good divorce is better than a bad marriage." He looked up at me and said, "You got that one right."

I said, "I do?"

He laughed and said, "Yup, you got that one exactly right. A good divorce is better than a bad marriage."

I paused, and I looked at him, and I said, "Well, you look like you probably have some experience."

He said, "My wife here and I, we've been married sixty-two years."

"Well, I have to ask you," I said. "What's the key to being married for sixty-two years?"

She grabbed his arm, leaned over, and said, "I got this one." I thought that might be the key.

"All right," I said, "you tell me."

"This is it," she said. "Let the other person be who they are, and put up with it."

That's good advice, folks. I've used it as a toast at many weddings since that day. Let the other person be who they are and put up with it.

Does that mean that you have to put up with it if they're a jerk? No. It just means that you're kidding yourself if you think you can change someone.

Some people get married. The wife has it in her mind, "I can change him." Seven or eight years later, she's complaining to her friends, "I couldn't change him." Let's be clear about this: you were an idiot to think you could change him in the first place.

People change when they want to, not when you want them to. They are never going to change simply because you have a different view of them in your mind. People will change when it's important for them to change, for their own reasons, not because they got married or because it would make you happy.

So have a realistic look at the other person and understand they're probably going to be who they are forever. If you don't understand that, and you aren't willing to put up with it, you're going to have to reassess your relationship. That's how it is. They just are who they are. Learn to put up with it, enjoy it, and make a joke of it if you can. Or perhaps it's time for you to move on.

One key to any good relationship, whether it be with friends or your spouse or even your kids, is good communications. You can fix almost anything that you're willing to talk about.

I see many relationships destroyed by conversations that are never had. It's been said that the number-one cause for divorce is money problems. These days there's a popular name for it, which I actually like: *financial infidelity*. Couples lead their own financial lives and never talk about how they spend their money or even about how much money they make.

You have couples who are hiding their finances from each other, not being honest, lying, buying things and keeping them hidden in the closet or in the car trunk—guys with a new set of golf clubs, a woman with a new dress. That's dishonest.

Many relationships could be fixed if people would just sit down and have a conversation. I think that's one of the problems with much of today's technology: we've forgotten how to sit down face-to-face, look each other in the eye, and have a conversation. It's easy to lie when you're typing with your thumbs. It's not easy to lie when you're looking each other in the eye.

One of the most important things that you can do is learn to talk to each other about everything that's going on in your life. Couples get in trouble, and they go to counseling. What do the counselors have them do? Typically they have couples sit face-to-face and talk to each other. Really.

What if you just started talking to each other at the very beginning and kept on talking to each other? When my wife and I have a challenge, we talk it out. I'm one of those guys who won't go to bed mad. I won't do it. I want to get it worked out.

If we have to say up to 2:00 or 3:00 in the morning and fight about it, well, then we're going to stay up, because I want it done, I want it worked out, I want it over. I don't like things to fester and get worse and worse, because things grow over time. That's how resentment gets bigger and bigger, when it all could have been solved just by two people willing to talk.

I also want to talk about fighting. I've talked to couples who say, "We never fight." That's sad. I think couples *should* fight. I'm not talking about a physical fight. I'm talking about a knock-down, drag-out, verbal altercation where everybody gets it said. I think that's essential.

Two people who pretend not to fight—either they're people who don't have an opinion, don't care enough about the opinion to speak up about it, or are practicing avoidance and keeping it all bottled up. But if you keep it all bottled up, it will eventually build to a boil and spill over, and you have a problem then. I think good, healthy disagreement is essential in any relationship with your friends, with your boss, with your coworkers, and certainly with your spouse.

How can you expect to share every aspect of your life with someone and never have a disagreement? It doesn't make sense to me, and it doesn't sound healthy to me either. I believe a good argument is a good thing to have. I will also tell you that when you're having that argument as a married couple and you have children, it's OK for them to see you. You need to role-play for them, to be an example for them on how to have an argument.

Do you know how to have an argument? Most people don't. When you're having an argument, that's called good verbal communications. You keep the argument about the subject. You make sure that it's always on topic. You never reduce the argument to personal attacks. It's not about who you are. It's about what you've done. It's about what has happened. It's about a topic.

As long as two people fight fair, you should show your children what it looks like, so they can eventually know how to have an argument with each other—including brothers and sisters. Kids fight. Teach them how to do it correctly.

The way to fight correctly is to stay on topic. Don't let it go down to the level where you are attacking each other personally. That's not what an argument should be about. It should always be about *something*. As long as you're talking about something, and you come to a mutual agreement, that's a good argument, and that's what you should be showing your kids.

Now let's move into how to be a good parent. As I've mentioned, I wrote a best-selling book on parenting called *Your Kids Are Your Own Fault*. That's probably the book that got the most pushback in my history, because parents don't like to be told that their kids are their fault.

I did a debate on a radio show with a woman who was disgusted by my use of *fault*, that I could dare say kids were the fault of the parents. Well, we could get real basic with that and say, "How did you end up having kids to begin with?" It seems to me that what you did to create the kid might have been your own fault. Unless you just accidentally had that happen, I can't see any other way to have gotten the child.

Finally I asked the woman, "Would you like it better if I reworded the title of this book to be *Your Children Are Your Responsibility*? The way your children turn out are the result of what you've done for them and to them in their lives."

She said, "I have no problem with that."

"Well, ma'am," I said, "that's called *fault*."

I've already talked a lot about fault in this book, but fault is a result. If your kids turn out to be good, amazing people who live lives of honesty and integrity and are responsible, you know what? That's your fault. If they turn out to be a mess, that could be your fault too.

Here's where we mess up as parents. We don't understand the goal of parenting. The goal of parenting is independence. Your goal, as a mama and a daddy, is for them to go away. If your kids live with you at the age of thirty, you did not achieve your goal, and in my opinion, you are a failure as a parent.

How's that for politically incorrect? I'm calling you a failure as a parent, because if the goal of parenting is independence, your job was to teach them how to be independent. Your job was to give them the skills to go away and survive and thrive all on their own.

Here's where the whole thing breaks down. We don't prepare our children with the skills to do that.

Let me ask you this question. What does it take for a thirty-five-year-old man or woman to be successful and make it in the world today? What skills does it take?

It seems to me that they would have to understand some basics, like how money works, how to pay your bills. They would need to understand what a work ethic is: how to show up on time, how to do a good job, how to give it all you've got every single day. They would need to understand about relationships, how to communicate, how to have an argument. They would need to know some basic things about sex, I would believe; otherwise they're going to have a lot of issues. They're going to need to know a lot of the things that you know now as an adult. Whose job is it to make sure they learn those things? It's your job. You're the parent.

It is your job to prepare your child to go out and live as an adult, to make sure they have those skills. So here's what I would like you to do if you have children. Again, get a sheet of paper, and write down everything a thirty-five-year-old is going to need to know in order to be successful in life.

After you have your list, I want you to ask your-self, are you teaching your children these princi-ples? Are you teaching them these skills? Create the perfect thirty-five-year-old in your mind and work backwards, because it is your job to start teaching those skills from the time they are born.

I've always used this example. If you decided to build a house and you'd bought the lot, would you do this? You back your truck up to the lumberyard and say, "Oh, I'll just take a pile of lumber over there, and give me a whole bunch of electrical wire, and I'll take a couple of sinks and a couple of toilets, and let me see . . . yup, throw a roll of carpet on there, and some wood flooring." Then you back the truck up to the lot, and you dump it all out there. You stand back, look at all that stuff lying in the middle of the vacant lot, fold your arms, and say, "Boy, I hope that works out." Now that's stupid, isn't it?

That's how we parent. We have all this fun cre-ating a child—talking about how our child will turn out, what they'll be when they grow up, all the poten-tial they have, all the opportunities they will have. Then we fold our arms, look at that baby in the crib, and in essence say, "Boy, I hope that works out."

If you wanted to build a house, you might buy all that stuff, but you'd have a plan. You would have a blueprint to make sure that you ended up with what you had in mind. Why don't you do that as a parent? Why don't you have a plan? Why don't you have a blueprint? Why don't you know in advance what you're going to do to make sure it ends up the way you want?

Why not? All you have to do is decide in advance what your child needs to know and make sure you teach it.

Typically in society these days, when your child makes a mistake, you defend your child against the school system, against any other parent, but you don't take responsibility for the fact that you didn't give them the skills to work through that particular matter.

When adult children move back in with their parents, the first place parents go to lay the blame is to the school system. We love to blame the school system. Are school systems to blame? Yeah, they are. They are making a lot of mistakes these days. I think school systems could be much better, I really do, but you know the way to make a school system better? Parental involvement. PTA meetings are nearly empty these days. Parents can't be bothered with going. Don't expect a school system to get better if you don't show up at a PTA meeting. Don't expect teachers to improve if you don't voice your opinion.

That's a shame, but let me make this clear. When your thirty-year-old can't make it in the real world and moves back into their room, they're not moving back into their schoolroom. They're moving back into their bedroom. It's not the school who will ultimately be responsible for that child. It's you.

You are the parent. If you want to make sure that your kid has the skills and knows what they need to know to be successful, send them to school. Be involved in the school system, but ultimately understand that whether the school system does its job or not, it is still your responsibility to teach your kids what they need to know in order to be successful.

The best thing you can do for your kids is spend time with them—some real time with them, time that's involved with them. I'm not talking about sitting on the couch side-by-side playing a video game or watching television. I'm talking about an exchange of ideas, which means you have to communicate with your kids. You have to talk to them.

Your kids will reach the point where they don't want to talk to you. I don't care. Talk to them anyway. It's not up to the kid. One thing that's happened in our country is that we believe families are democracies where kids get a vote. Kids don't get a vote. They're kids. Families are absolute monarchies. You are responsible. You are the king and the queen of your house. What you say goes. You have to run your home in that way in order to make your kids feel more comfortable with who they are. Kids need someone to be in charge. They don't need another friend. They have friends.

You're going to teach them what real friendship is. You're going to know who their friends are. You're going to make sure that they have good, high-quality friends around them. That's your job as a parent. You don't need to be their friend. You need to be their parent, and the best thing you can do to know your child is to talk to your child and be involved with your child.

Next thing is you have to be tough on your kids. You have to discipline them. Let me tell you what *discipline* means. *Discipline* does not mean *punish*. It means that you establish a code of conduct within your house and your family that says what is acceptable and what is not acceptable. Then you manage your family by that code of conduct.

The military has a code of conduct. Churches have a code of conduct. That's the way most institutions act. That's the way most businesses behave. They have a code of conduct that says, "This is acceptable within the walls of this business. This is what will fly; this is what will not fly."

Have you established that in your own home? That's what discipline is. Unfortunately, we believe that disciplining your child is punishing your child.

Here's the deal. You establish a code of conduct, disciplines to live by. You communicate those disciplines, you talk them through, and you show your children how to live that way and be that way. You also communicate the consequences of what happens when they don't live that way. If you've done a good job with those things, you don't have to punish very much.

If you ask the typical parent today, "What do you spend most of your time doing?" many would say they spend most of their time punishing their children for misbehaving. To me, that doesn't even make sense. You should have spent the bulk of your time teaching your child how to behave, giving them the skills that they needed in order to behave, and showing them what behaving looks like. When you do that, you really don't have to spend much time punishing them for not behaving.

It seems to me we have things backwards when it comes to teaching our children codes of conduct, and certainly when it comes to punishing.

When it comes to teenagers, you need to know the only thing that will give you hope is that they will eventually grow out of it.

When one of my sons was fifteen years old, that's all I could cling to. At that age, he was bigger than I was. He stood up to me one day and said, "Dad, I don't have to listen to you anymore. I'm bigger than you are."

I smiled and said, "Yes, you are, son. You're bigger than I am, but I'm meaner than you are, I have all the money, and I know where you sleep."

He paused, looked at me, said, "You're right," turned around, and walked off.

When my other son was about that age, I said, "Son, I love you. I can't stand you right now, but I love you. That's all you need to remember. I don't care whether you love me right now or not. I don't even care whether you like me. What matters is I'm your dad, and I love you, and whether you like it or not, you're going to listen to me, and you're going to do what I know is best for you."

I don't see a lot of parents with enough of a pair to do that these days. We acquiesce too quickly to our kids. When I see a ten-year-old little girl with an elaborate iPhone, I know who's running that household. It's not mommy and daddy. That little girl is running that household.

When I see a two-year-old throwing a tantrum in the middle of a busy restaurant, and mamas and daddies are shaking their heads or laughing it off and saying, "Oh, that's just how she is," that two-year-old is running that family.

Take charge of your family. It's going to be especially challenging for you when they are teenagers, but it's less challenging if you've done a good job beforehand. Don't let them slide when they're little kids, and then, when they've become teenagers and have some size on them and a better vocabulary, suddenly expect them to be perfect. You have to have done your work already.

Here's another thing I want to tell you about teenagers. When a teenager says they need you the least is when they absolutely need you the most. Remember that.

Another mistake that I see parents making these days: they reduce themselves to the level of the child. In the mall, I heard a daughter turn to the mother and say, "I hate you," and the mother said, "I hate you too."

How sad! First of all, a child shouldn't hear from the parent that the parent hates them. It shouldn't happen. You should love them no matter what. At least you should reinforce the idea that as a parent, you care about them, no matter what.

If you reduce yourself to playing, "I hate you," "No, I hate you," you're not a good mama or daddy. Your job is to love them when they hate you. It doesn't mean that you approve of what they've done. You can hate what they've done. You need to love them as a person.

Love for your child is unconditional. Approval is up for grabs, based on their behavior. You are responsible for judging their behavior, teaching them how to behave the right way in the right circumstance. You should also teach them what the wrong behavior is and impose consequences when you get it. That's your job as a parent.

Speaking of the word *hate* when it comes to teenagers, if your teenager at some point doesn't say to you, "I hate you," you're probably not doing your job as a parent. It is their job to hate you when they're teenagers. It's like they get paid to do it or something. They wake up at 8:00 in the morning, and they do it until they go to bed at night. Really, it's their career. So be tough. Don't listen to it. Understand they're going to grow out of it, but you have to do your job whether they like it or not.

I used to jokingly say that there are only three things you can do to help you get through the teenage years: put them in their room, lock the door, and feed them flounder and pancakes. Why flounder and pancakes? You can slide them under the door.

It's a lot like everything else I've talked about. You have to start with yourself. If you want to have good kids, if you want to teach them the skills they're going to need to know, you need to model that behavior for them. You need to be a person of integrity. It's impossible to tell your kids not to lie and then, when the phone rings and they answer it, turn around and mouth the words, "Tell them I'm not here." When you do that, you've taught your kids to lie. That's a lack of integrity. It's dishonest. You have modeled that behavior for them. You tell your kids not to cheat, but 25 percent of adults cheat on their taxes. I'm sure that discussion went on in a place where the kids could hear it.

You have to be the kind of person you want your child to become. Your children are always going to be reflections of who you are. What kind of person are you? Become the kind of person you would like for your children to become.

You also need to talk about what really matters in life and model that behavior for them. As I said at the beginning of this book, I have five core principles that I will never compromise, no matter what. My number-one principle is that your life is your own fault, and you have to be responsible for that life. When I wrote *Your Kids Are Your Own Fault*, I asked each of my grown sons to write a chapter for the book. I said, "I won't edit it, I won't correct the spelling, I won't do one thing for this chapter. What you write is what goes in the book. I want you to write a couple of pages about what it was like to grow up the son of Larry Winget."

Both of my boys—please read the book, it's the most important thing that I've ever done—turned in sheets of paper to me that were all about personal responsibility. When they had to face up to a real mistake they had made in their lives and accept that their behavior had consequences, they didn't come running to me. They stood tall and took it. They took the consequences of their behavior.

That's what they say they learned from me. I didn't encourage them to do that. I said, "Whatever you write is fine with me. You can write, 'My dad was a jerk.' Whatever you write is going in the book." That's what they chose to write.

That was a real moment of pride for me. I was very proud that I had at least been able to teach them that one thing.

One time, when I was going on a trip to give a long series of speeches, I was standing at my back door getting ready to go to the airport. My son, who was nineteen at the time, said, "Dad, I've yet to figure out why anybody would pay you to come talk to them."

"What a sweet thing for you to say, son."

"I mean it, Dad," he said. "I've heard your eighteen principles. I've heard you tell people how simple it all is. I've heard your number-one rule for life and business. Dad, I live with you. I know the real Larry Winget. I don't think you have it figured out. I'm the one who has life figured out."

"After all, son," I said, "you have just flunked out of your first semester of college, you've just totaled your car, and you just got fired. Obviously you have the answers. Tell me what the answer is."

"All right, Dad, here it is: when you mess up, big deal. Just admit it, fix it, and move on. Other than that, life's a party."

You know what? He's right. Have you ever messed up? Big deal. We all mess up. Everybody's always going to mess up. Big deal. Then he said what in my opinion was most critical: "Admit it." That's called *taking responsibility*. If that is the only thing I ever taught my two boys, then I was a pretty good daddy.

Admit it, fix it, clean up your own mess. What a great lesson to teach your kids. Clean up your own mess. You caused it, you're responsible for it, and move on.

Don't you wish that you could just tell some of the people in your life, "Move on, it's over. Get over it"? My son learned that somehow growing up with me.

Then he said something that I believe is absolutely critical to life as well. "Other than that, life's a party." We've forgotten to enjoy our lives. So those are the lessons my son learned from me.

I also will tell you this: if you want to help your kids be better, help them pick their role models. Then talk about why that person should be a role model. Earlier in this program, I mentioned a sort of hall of fame of people you admired, your role models, and what attributes that you wanted to model in your own life.

Do the same thing with your kids. Help them choose role models. Don't let their peer group pick role models for them. That's a big mistake. You are responsible. Talk to them about what you admire in certain political officials or world leaders or business leaders. Give them respect for those people based on something that they have seen that's being talked about.

There are also lots of people in your neighborhood that you should admire. Bring up those people: people they know, people they can hang around and find those qualities in so they will start to model that behavior in their own lives.

Talk about it when one of their friends does something that should be admired. Point out that attribute in one of their friends: "You know I like how your friend, Johnny, did this. He handled that really well. He took responsibility" or whatever it was. Talk about that behavior. Honor the things that you want to build in your child's life. Honor those things in the lives of other people.

Next, set really high expectations. I've learned that people will either live up to or down to what you expect of them. The more you expect of your child, the better they will do.

Then impose consequences. I know it's hard, but you should impose consequences when you do not get the behavior that you want.

I remember one time when one of my kids was twelve years old. He was a typical boy in every single way. If there was a rule, he was going to break it. If there was a limit, he would push it. He was that kind of kid. I sat him down, and I said, "Son."

"Let me interrupt you, Dad," he said. "Here's what I want you to do. This time just beat me. I don't need a speech."

I laughed and said, "You hate our little talks, don't you?"

"I hate these talks. This time I want you to beat me."

"Since you hate these talks so much," I said, "let's have a good one."

Boy, did he help me out. He made me a better parent. I figured out what he hated the most, and that was the consequence I imposed on him.

Impose the consequences that you know hurt the most. You know the best way to hurt a kid these days? Take away their gadget. That hurts. While you're doing that, ask yourself how young your child is and whether they really need that gadget to begin with.

I also think your kids need to be involved in sports, lots of activities. They need to learn what it's like to compete. We've reached this place in society where we no longer keep score. I think that's a shame, and I think you must seek out those teams that don't behave in that way.

We should not live in a society where everyone gets a trophy. We should teach kids how to lose. We should teach them how to win with honor and lose with dignity. That takes some failure along the way. Find yourself a team that your kids can play on where they can have a lot of fun, enjoy themselves, learn what it means to get knocked down and get back up, and learn what it means to win and what it means to lose.

We're not teaching our kids about failure these days. Amazingly, life is made up more of failure than it is of success. If we don't prepare our kids to lose, to fail from time to time, we have done them a disservice.

Again I ask you to get out a sheet of paper and write down your five core values: the principles that you will not compromise. This time do it in terms of your relationships. What's important to you? What five things will you not compromise?

If you're a parent, get out a second sheet of paper and write down the core values and principles for your children and how you will be as a parent.

6

The World:
A Reflection
of You

At this point we've talked about fixing you. We've talked about you and your business, you and your money, you and you relationships, you and your kids.

Now let's talk about you and the world as it exists today. The world has changed. We're supposed to be ready for change, but I don't believe that some of the changes we're going through right now are all that good. We're letting change get away from us. We are letting our citizens run amok, we're letting our government officials run amok, and we are letting our society as a whole run amok. We're going to have to get back in control. If we're going to save society as we know it, we are going to have to be better in our world.

The world is a reflection of its citizens. Just like every other area, everything reflects who we are. People want to blame the government, but the government is a reflection of who we have become.

You don't like the government? Look at yourself. This is who we are. If you think that the government has become entitled and gets to do whatever it wants, look around you. People have become entitled and think that they can do whatever they want.

If you look at your political officials, you need to understand they are us. We have allowed that to happen. Our government has become what we have allowed it to become. It always comes back to one thing: this is your fault. This is my fault. We created this government by voting them in.

You can sit back and say, "I didn't vote for them." Chances are you're right. You didn't vote for them. Very few people vote these days. Not nearly enough people do.

Every time I talk about voting, somebody will say, "Larry, you don't understand. Voting doesn't matter anymore." I understand the argument: some people believe their votes have been bought and sold and no one's individual vote matters. Please let me give you a word of advice. If you ever see me face-to-face, don't say that to me, because that ticks me off. Voting *does* matter. When you start convincing people that our individual votes don't matter, that's when you're going to see even fewer people going to the polls. This is a privilege we must exercise.

Only about 60 percent of the people who are eligible to vote are actually registered to vote, and on average only about 40 percent of those show up at any given election. That's just a darn shame. Regardless of which side you're on, at least be on a side. Know why you're on that side.

Too few people show up at the polls. If you proudly sit back and say, "At least I didn't vote for them. I didn't vote at all," you're an idiot. You allowed this to happen by not participating. You have no right to gripe if you didn't participate.

So many people who want to complain, and yet they didn't participate. Participation is absolutely key. I believe every single person should get out and vote.

You'll say, "They're all crooks. I'm not voting for the lesser of two evils." That's a stupid thing to say. It's *always* going to come down to the lesser of two evils. That's what it is. Every time you go to the grocery store, that's the lesser of two evils. We're always picking the one that is least offensive to us, maybe not the one who's the best.

By the way, the one who's the least offensive is the one who's the best.

So go vote for the best out of the two, and don't argue about the two-party system. This is the game we have right now. You have to play with the game that you're given, folks. Don't opt out of it. Participate in it.

Actually, if you voted in the lesser of two evils, and then next time somebody was up for election, you voted in the lesser of two evils, do you not understand that eventually we would have a less evil government? That would mean it had gotten better. Participate. Always vote every single time.

Teach your kids the importance of voting. Don't be a parent who sits back and says, "It doesn't matter." It matters. We still get to vote. Remember, we have kids that go overseas and have fought and died for your right to do that. Don't dishonor them by choosing not to participate. Be a good citizen.

Speaking of being a good citizen, think of yourself as a citizen. Think of yourself as a contributor to what we have become as a country. This mean that your contribution every single day when you get up and go to work matters. Start knowing that it matters.

If you're a person who always has taken money from the government, if you're one of the takers and not the makers, don't make that your goal. Don't make that your life's goal, always to be on the take. Be a person who contributes. You'll feel much better about yourself knowing that you have done your best to make this world and this society a better place.

Most of you reading this book are probably here in America. You need to be proud of that fact. We need to honor our country and what it took to build our country. I am a flag waver, and when I see school systems that are willing to take down the flag because some students find it offensive to others, that bothers me. I don't like that.

We should honor our flag and proudly salute it and say the Pledge of Allegiance every single time. Is that politically incorrect? I don't care. I'm a proud American, and I don't care where you're from. Be proud of where you're from.

It's not perfect. Nothing is perfect. It might be a mess. I believe we are in a mess right now, but it is part of my job as a citizen to get up and do my part to make it better every single day.

How do I do my part? First of all, by knowing what's going on. It is my job to stay current about what is going on. I am amazed at the people every single day who wake up and say, "I don't watch the news."

Last week in my gym I actually heard a guy say, "I don't watch television. I certainly don't watch the news. Everything I know about what's going on in the world, I get from my Facebook thread." I nearly blew the water out of my nose as I heard this guy say that.

First of all, never brag about how stupid and uninformed you are. Nobody ought to know that about you. Besides, if you are not aware of it at this point, much of the "news" that shows up on social media is made-up stories.

Do a little research to make sure that you're informed about what's really going on, and don't buy into just one talking head. I know people who say a particular news channel is all a load of crap, and it's all made up. Then they'll say it doesn't matter whether you're on the right or the left, you have your favorite news channel. My suggestion is that you watch a little bit of all of it, and then you do some research, and you become an informed voter. You become an informed citizen, so you're not just following the pack.

Don't be a "sheeple." Don't be like everybody else. Do your research. Know what's going on in the world. Stay informed. Don't think that it's OK to just be ignorant and uninformed. It's not OK.

If you're ignorant, you can't stay relevant in the marketplace. You can't stay relevant in the work-place. You can't stay relevant in society. And when you figure out what's going on in society, it is your job to have an opinion about it. When you cast your vote, that's your opinion. Too many people sit back and only complain about what's going on when they don't really know.

When I see people saying and posting stupid things, I believe it's my job as a guy who has a pair to make sure they understand that they're full of it and they don't know what they're talking about. Then I will quote the real news story. I will show them the research that I've done.

I know what I'm talking about. In the last twenty-five years, I've read over 4,500 books. I don't know anybody who's read any more books than I have. Most people can't figure out how to read one book after they graduate from high school.

Is it because I have so much time on my hands? No, it's because I have a commitment to always improving myself, because I understand if I want to the world to be better, if I want business to be better, if I want my business to be better, if I want my life to be better, *I* have to be better.

My world is a reflection of who I am. I have a pretty good life. Why? Not because it was given to me, because I worked my butt off to get it. I improved my skills, I improved my level of learning, so when I bring an opinion into the marketplace, it's an educated opinion.

Ask yourself right now: do you have an educated opinion, or is it an uninformed opinion? Be honest with yourself. Don't just tell me, "Yes, it's an informed opinion," because I will say, "Where did you get that opinion?" If you tell me that you got it by watching one channel and only one channel, that's not a well-balanced opinion. That is a narrow focus.

I read as much as I can from works by as many people as I can. I read people I believe are idiots. You know why? Because it strengthens my point of view. I need something to disagree with to confirm what I do agree with. I do my best to stay current and informed. Are you doing that? You owe it to yourself, you owe it to your family, and you certainly owe it to your country to do that.

Let's talk about what's happened in society that got us to the point where people are uninformed, where they feel entitled to having people take care of them, where they've stopped doing for themselves and want everybody to do something for them.

We used to be a pull-yourself-up-by-your-bootstraps kind of country. We used to be a society that took care of its own and didn't look to someone else to take care of them; certainly we didn't look to the government. We did it on our own. That's who we were—the greatest generation.

These were people who worked through the Depression, the Great Depression, not the few recessions we've had. They did it by hard work, getting better at who they were and better at what they did. They built things. They didn't expect someone to come in and take care of them. What happened to those people?

I'll tell you what happened to them. Those people went out and had kids. They wanted their kids not to have it as tough as they did, and they pampered their kids just a little bit. Those kids became the boomers. Some of the boomers did a really good job; we worked really hard. But then the boomers went through the sixties and the seventies. It started with the beatnik generation, and then there was the hippie generation.

Then we got into self-actualization, and it was "I'm OK, you're OK." That's not true. Chances are, I'm not so good, and you're probably an idiot. I'm not OK, and you're not OK. That's the reality, but we started believing all that stuff, and then we had the self-help movement.

I love the self-help movement. I am a part of that movement. But we bastardized the entire concept of self-help. It used to be about empowerment, but we turned empowerment into entitlement. It used to mean that you can have whatever you are willing to work hard enough to make happen in your life. You can create in your life what you believe you deserve.

We turned that "I deserve more by going out and working for it" into "I deserve more; somebody should do it for me." We lost our way, and we have to find our way again.

The boomers had kids, and they wanted it to be better for their kids, and they required less and less of them. They allowed them to think that someone would take care of them. In fact we did take care of them, and we created the millennials.

Again, if you are a millennial reading this book, I'm not putting down your entire generation. I know many of you do a great job and are strong entrepreneurs. Our future really is in your hands. You are the people who will be creating jobs in the future, and you'll be hiring boomers. I'm great with that. Boomers need jobs, because they didn't take care of themselves along the way, and now they're going into retirement with no money. I hope millennials will go out there and create lots of businesses that will hire all these old guys and put them to work.

I'm not talking about you if this doesn't apply to you. If you truly are the exception, that's fine, but we need to be concerned, and here's why. Every generation gets a little weaker. Every generation expects a little more. Every generation turns to someone else to take care of them just a little bit more.

Now the millennials are having children. My concern is for them. Are we going to expect even less of them, or are we going to step up to the plate and require more from them?

I hope that's the case. I hope we turn this thing around so we can create the next generation. I don't know what they're going to be called, but I hope we create a generation that doesn't expect other people to take care of them.

I was out with some friends recently, and I was on a rant like this, talking about all the people who expect to be taken care of. These were some good, liberal friends of mine, and they turned to me and said, "Larry, you have no interest in taking care of people, do you?"

"No, I don't," I said. "I have no interest in taking care of people. My interest lies in teaching people to take care of themselves."

I want to teach people to take care of themselves. I hope that's what you want. I hope that's what parents want. I hope that's what we do with this next generation. I hope millennials will learn to take care of themselves. I hope that boomers too will very quickly understand they have to take care of themselves. They have to turn their lives around right now. There's no time to be wasted. They have to start saving more, earning more, changing their lifestyles. They have to be smarter. They have to reduce expectations for help from everyone else and turn to themselves as the solution.

If you want the world to get better, you must be become more involved. As I've said, your kids will get better. Your family will get better. Your government will get better as well.

When people complain to me about the government, I always ask, "What are you doing about it?" It starts with voting, but voting is just the bare minimum. What else are you doing? Have you ever written your congressman? Have you actually reached out to the people who represent you and said, "This is what I want you to vote on; it's important to me"? Have you? Why not? Are you just sitting back and letting it happen?

People are all pro-charity. When they say we should give to charity, I ask, "Have you done something about it? Have you written a check?" That's what it comes down to.

How do you become more involved with government? It starts at the local level. It might start even with your local homeowners' association. You need to show up and learn how to speak up and have a discussion. Get good at speaking up. Know how to disagree. Know how to move toward resolution. Go to local party meetings. It's easy to do. Talk to them about what's important to you.

Part of being a good citizen is being informed about a topic, having an opinion, knowing how to articulate that opinion, and showing up and speaking up for what is important to you. Again, it's knowing what your core values are. Once you know what these values are and speak up for them and live them, your life will change. It works the same way in your family, your business, and in your government.

Our political leaders get a lot of media exposure. But it tends to focus only on their clay feet. We only see how fallible they are. We focus only on all the things that they've done wrong, and we forget all of the things that they've done right.

Folks, everybody messes up. If Abraham Lincoln were to run for the presidency today, he would never get it, because he went bankrupt, because he didn't have a college education. How could anybody ever run government who doesn't have a college education?

But there was a time when we focused more on a person's leadership capabilities than we did on all the things we focus on now. People ask me, "Larry, why don't you run for political office?" Folks, I can tell you right now, you don't want Larry Winget to run for president. People talk about skeletons in their closet. I have a warehouse full of skeletons.

Now I am quick to admit what they are, but that makes me a real person. Why do you expect your politicians to be anything other than real people? I don't care when somebody has made a mistake. I wouldn't hold you accountable for the rest of your life for a mistake you made when you were younger. I wouldn't hold you accountable for the rest of your life for a mistake you made today if you took responsibility, were sincerely sorry, and moved on by making sure you didn't do that again.

Why won't you cut today's politicians and political figures the same amount of slack that you would want people to cut you? Why do you expect perfection? Because somehow we've gotten to the point where we want everybody in a leadership position to be perfect.

When you look back through business history, there are lots of great business leaders who were horrible business leaders at one point, but they learned along the way. How did they learn? The same way you learn, the same way your kids learn, the same way we all learn—by making mistakes.

It's OK to make a mistake. It's not OK not to learn from that mistake. We have people who could be great leaders if we would just cut them some slack and allow them to participate.

Like in all the other sections, I'm asking you to be politically incorrect by becoming politically involved. That leads me to the list. You know the list—the list where I ask you to establish the five things you won't compromise when it comes to your government. I want you to take a few minutes and write those things down.

Let me give you some suggestions. Start out by being better informed. Then participate by voting, and then have realistic expectations for your elected officials and for your government. Remember, fix yourself first. It's not fair to expect a government to live within its budget if you're not living within yours. Your government is a reflection of who you are.

Those would be the three I would suggest. If you want to use them, that's fine, which means you only have to come up with two more. But take a minute and write down the five things you will not compromise when it comes to your government and this society.

I hope you've enjoyed this book. We are moving toward the end. We are moving toward a graduation of sorts, one that will move you from where you have been in your life to where you would like to be, which begins with a commencement.

Graduation ceremonies always have a commencement speech. It means graduates are about to commence a new walk in life.

You're about to do the very same thing. You're going to graduate from the Larry Winget Politically Incorrect Success System and start your life anew.

Let me give you a bit of a commencement address with a few words of advice I have for you, just a couple of ideas that you'll want to use as you move forward.

Remember the importance of respect. *Respect* means that you respect yourself enough, that you always give yourself the best shot at doing anything, that you give yourself every opportunity, and you take advantage of every opportunity, that you show up trying to do your very best when given the chance to do your very best.

That's personal respect. That's where self-respect comes from. That's where self-esteem comes from. I can't give you self-esteem. No one can. I can't give you self-respect. No one can do that, because the root word there is *self*. You have to respect yourself enough to give yourself your best.

You need to respect others. You need to respect the people you work for, your boss. You might be saying, "My boss is an idiot." I don't care. Your boss might be an idiot, but your boss is your boss, and your boss is paying you to do a job. Respect your boss enough to do that job.

Respect the company you work for, because they pay you. Does that mean they're perfect? No, and if you hate it that much, go find a different company. Don't stay and complain about it and make everybody else miserable. Don't be a whiner. Don't be a complainer.

Respect the company that pays you. Don't bite the hand that feeds you. Be realistic. I know they aren't perfect, but it is dumb to believe that you can give a company and their customers the best when you constantly are bad-mouthing them. Respect the people you work for. Respect your customers.

Remember an old line by Earl Nightingale: "All of the money you're ever going to have is currently in the hands of someone else." In business we call that someone else the *customer*. Respect that customer, and do your best for them.

Next is this. Don't ever skip the basics. You will be known for the basics. You showed up on time. You worked hard. You were the kind of person that others could count on. You did what you said you would do. You did it when you said you would do it. You did it the way you said you would do it. You remember that's my number-one rule for life and business? That's a basic, folks; the little things that most people take for granted. Don't be that person. Never take those little things for granted.

Learn to smile at people. My dad used to tell me, "Larry, smile. It don't cost nothing." It wasn't very good grammar, but it was a good message. Smile, it don't cost nothing. It'll make people like you more. Does that matter? Actually it does. Likability has its rewards.

Learn to look people in the eye. Shoot them straight. Communicate well with them. Shake their hand. Be a person that other people want to be around. Be a person that attracts the right kind of people in their life.

Next is this. Be worth more than you cost. This is a great rule for business. If you want to earn more money in your life, be worth more money. How do you become worth more? By looking at what you do every single day and figuring out a way to do it a little bit better, to do it a little bit faster and a little bit cheaper, and to do it in a way that other people will see more value in what you do.

Look at what you do and say, "How can I add more value so that my worth is much more than my cost?" Remember, you're always an expense. Your goal is to make yourself worth more than what you cost.

Next, understand this. It's an old adage in the personal-development industry. I heard it first from Zig Ziglar. "Everything in your life gets better when you get better." If you want your life to get better, *you* get better. Become better informed. Improve your life skills. Improve your knowledge base. Improve your attitude. Improve your work ethic.

Now ask yourself this: am I teaching my kids those same basics? If you want your kids to get better, become a better parent. If you want a better family, be a better person in that family. If you want better relationships, be a better friend. You'll have better friends. Be a better spouse. You'll have a better spouse. If you want a better world, be a better citizen.

Everything that's going on in your life is a reflection of you. If you want everything in your life to get better, you must get better.

My next piece of advice is this: don't spend major time on minor things. Most things that take up the bulk of your day could probably be skipped with few or no consequences. This comes down to knowing what your priorities are. What's really important? What's the most important thing for me to do? Know that in advance.

When you have clear priorities and core values, it will not only help you manage your time better, it will help you manage your life better. Make sure you're not spending all your time and energy on the minor things in life. Instead focus on what's really important.

Then there's this: Don't be a wimp. Know what you believe in. Know what you stand for and stand up for it. Do it with your kids, your coworkers, your friends, and your government. In other words, grow a pair.

Don't make any excuses. Take responsibility. If you did it, own up to it. Don't be a person who ducks responsibility. If you made a mistake, admit you made a mistake. Remember what my son said. "Admit it, fix it, and move on."

Stop caring what others say and think about you. Live your life according to your core values. When you do that, you will be a happier person, you will be a better person, and things in your life will go better.

Last is this: always have a plan. Too many people have a dream. Too many people have a goal. Very few people have a plan. You need a plan for your family, you need a plan for your kids, you need a plan for your money, you need a plan for your business, and you need a plan for your life. Know what you want, and figure out the steps it will take for you to get there, and then when you wake up in the morning, go to work.

All right. I've given you some ideas on how you can start to live a different kind of life, one that is more in alignment with who you really are and what you believe, one that will leave you with much more success and much more happiness.

How will you know you made it? When people ask me how I'm doing, I always respond with this: "It's good to be Larry Winget."

I've had plenty of times in my life when I wouldn't have been able to say that, but it got to be good to be Larry Winget when I started living my life the way I've been talking about, when I started living it according to my core values.

Ask yourself right now: is it good to be you all the time? If it's not, I've given you all the steps that you need to take so you'll be able to say, "It's good to be me."

Then remember this. At the end of the day, if you can say I laughed more than I cried, I made a solid contribution through my efforts, I'm known as a person of integrity, and I've told the people in my life I love them, it's been a pretty good day.

I hope you've enjoyed this book. I've given you my very best. If you want to find out more about who I am and what I do, please go online. Look me up at larrywinget.com. You'll find my books and all the other things I have to offer. You can also follow me on YouTube, and you can go to any bookstore and look up any of my books. They'll have them. You can follow me on Facebook at the Larry Winget fan page, on Twitter @Larry Winget. I'm an easy guy to find.